Skills for the 21st Century in Latin America and the Caribbean

Skills for the 21st Century in Latin America and the Caribbean

Cristian Aedo
Ian Walker

THE WORLD BANK
Washington, D.C.

ISBN (paper): 978-0-8213-8971-3
ISBN (electronic): 978-0-8213-8935-5
DOI: 10.1596/978-0-8213-8971-3

Cover photo: Dieter Telemans/Panos
Cover design: Naylor Design

Library of Congress Cataloguing-in-Publication Data has been applied for.

Contents

Boxes

Figures

Contents

Tables

Preface

There is growing interest, worldwide, in the link between education systems and the production of skills that are valued in the labor market. With growth stagnating and unemployment soaring in much of the world, educators are being asked to focus more on producing skills that feed into labor productivity and support the sustainable growth of employment and incomes.

This timely volume contributes important new findings on the dynamics of education systems and labor market outcomes in Latin America and the Caribbean (LAC). It analyzes an important recent shift in labor market trends in LAC: the first decade of the 21st century has witnessed a marked decline in the earnings premia for university and secondary education. This, in turn, is contributing to reduced income inequality across the region. The recent trend contrasts with the sharp rise in tertiary earnings premia that was observed in the 1990s and that helped to reinforce high levels of income inequality in the region at that time.

The authors—a team of education and social protection and labor market economists from the Human Development Department of the World Bank's LAC Region—document this trend through a rigorous analysis of household survey datasets from a dozen countries over the last two decades. They then reflect on the ramifications of the observed shift towards lower earnings premia, asking whether it is good news or bad news for the region.

They conclude that the answer is likely to be a bit of each. On the one hand, the supply and demand analysis presented in chapter three demonstrates that declining premia are related to dramatic increases in the relative supply of skilled labor (in particular at the secondary level). The authors also present time series data from the PISA test (now undertaken in nine countries in the region) showing that the quality of learning outcomes in LAC has been maintained, and even slightly improved, during this process of aggressive expansion. To have achieved such a large expansion of education in so little time, without affecting overall quality of learning achievement, is commendable. And, as noted above, the resulting reduction in earnings premia has contributed to improved income distribution patterns across the region. All this is good news.

But there are also negative connotations. The analysis of the PISA data shows that the stability of learning achievement in the region's expanding education system owes much to improving age-grade correspondence, which has limited scope to continue. Meanwhile, the quality of learning within specific grade levels has not been improving. At the same time, decomposition analyses suggest that the region has experienced a worrying drop in the relative demand for skilled labor. This contrasts with other regions, in particular East Asia, which are absorbing more highly skilled new entrants into their labor force without any decline in earnings premia. An analysis of the underlying causes of these differences raises worrying questions about trends in the quality and relevance of the skills being produced in LAC, which could affect the region's long term growth prospects.

Detailed analysis of trends in the skill content of Latin American jobs presented in chapter five shows that the region is not expanding in sectors which demand "new economy" skills. This suggests that, faced with constraints in the availability of relevant skills, firms might be limiting their choice of products and technologies to second-best options, at the expense of their competitive edge.

The authors recommend that, having achieved very large increases in secondary and tertiary enrollment, the region should now focus on improving the quality of its education systems and the pertinence of education curricula for the needs of the labor market. At age 15, the learning achievement of the average Latin American student still lags two years behind his or her OECD contemporary. That is a huge difference that, if unchallenged, will continue to undermine the region's competitiveness.

The study opens up an important agenda for future research. While the evidence presented on the trends in education earnings premia is clear, the conclusions about the causes and significance of those trends are largely based on suggestive evidence for a limited number of countries, and are not definitive because of data limitations. The findings call for further in-depth analysis of the nature of skill mismatches, to inform policies that can strengthen the region's future economic growth by enhancing the productivity and earnings potential of the workforce.

Keith Hansen
Director, Human Development Department
Latin America and the Caribbean Region
The World Bank

About the Authors

Cristian Aedo is a Senior Education Economist at the Europe and Central Asia Human Development Sector, the World Bank. He has published numerous articles on social sectors in Latin America and the Caribbean. He holds an M.A. and Ph.D. in Economics from the University of Minnesota, United States.

Ian Walker has been Lead Economist in the Latin America and the Caribbean Region Social Protection team at the World Bank since 2005. He is the author of studies on social protection, nutrition, and demand for public services, and he has led development policy lending focused on strengthening human development outcomes through better accountability in the Andean Region. Before joining the World Bank, he was Director of ESA Consultores in Honduras. He served as Chief Economic Adviser to the Maduro administration; led the team developing Honduras's Millennium Development Corporation program; and completed studies on a wide range of development issues in Central and South America, North Africa, the Middle East, and Central Asia. He holds a master's degree in Economics and Modern History from Oxford University, United Kingdom.

Acknowledgments

Skills for the 21st Century in Latin America and the Caribbean is the product of a team effort by the Latin America and the Caribbean Region Education and Social Protection units of the World Bank, co-led by Cristian Aedo and Ian Walker, the lead authors of this report. Background papers were prepared by Tim Gindling with Camilo Bohórquez, Sergio Rodriguez, and Romero Barreto Rocha; Ana Maria Oviedo and Gregory Veramendi; Cristian Aedo and Javier Luque; Pablo Acosta; Guillermo Cruces and Leonardo Gaspirini; Rita Almeida and Jaime Jesus; Ken Dodge, Nancy Guerra, and Ian Walker; and Cristian Aedo and John Middleton. Mary Downing and Lerick Kebeck provided invaluable logistical and administrative support.

The team particularly wishes to acknowledge the important contribution made to the conceptualization of this study during 2009 by Kathy Terrell. Her untimely death was a great loss to the project. We hope we have done justice to her ideas in this report.

The team received valuable feedback through a rich consultation and peer review process. The team values the ongoing support and technical inputs from the regional Chief Economist, Augusto de la Torre; Deputy Chief Economist, Francisco Ferreira; and Senior Economist, Jamele Rigolini. Insightful and constructive comments were received from peer reviewers

Carolina Sanchez, Amit Dar, Emanuela di Gropello, Jesko Hentschel, and John Giles, as well as from many other colleagues at the concept review and subsequent stages.

The findings, interpretations, and conclusions expressed in this document are those of the authors and do not necessarily reflect the views of the Executive Directors of the World Bank, the governments they represent, or the counterparts consulted or engaged with during the study process.

Vice President:	Pamela Cox
Regional Chief Economist:	Augusto de la Torre
Sector Director:	Keith Hansen
Sector Managers:	Helena Ribe and Chingboon Lee
Project Coteam Leaders:	Cristian Aedo and Ian Walker

Abbreviations

CEDLAS	Centro de Estudios Distributivos Laborales y Sociales
CEV	classical errors-in-variables
DOT	*Dictionary of Occupational Titles*
GDP	gross domestic product
LAC	Latin America and the Caribbean
MERCOSUR	Southern Common Market; Mercado Común del Sur
MxFLS	Mexican Family Life Survey
OECD	Organisation for Economic Co-operation and Development
OLS	ordinary least squares
O*NET	*Occupational Information Network*
PISA	Program for International Student Assessment
PPP	purchasing power parity
SAR	special administrative region
SEDLAC	Socieconomic Database for Latin America and the Caribbean
SERCE	Second Regional Comparative and Explanatory Study

TVET   technical vocational education and training
UNESCO   United Nations Educational, Scientific and Cultural
                Organization
USDOL/ETA   Employment and Training Administration of the
                U.S. Department of Labor

CHAPTER 1

Introduction and Summary

In the aftermath of a global economic crisis that left Latin America and the Caribbean (LAC) relatively unscathed, policy makers are refocusing their attention on the region's medium-term growth and development strategy. Amid optimistic talk of the possibility of a Latin American decade, the challenge of improving the performance of the region's labor markets once again looms large. Enhancing productivity growth, increasing earnings, and improving other dimensions of job quality, such as employment stability and social protection, are returning to center stage in policy debates. A central question policy makers must address in this context is how to maximize the future productivity and earnings gains from the region's accelerating investment in education.

The good news is that, across the region, income distribution is improving and poverty is declining. Improved relative earnings for the low-skilled are an important part of the story. But the other side of the same coin is that, in many LAC labor markets, education earnings premiums (the additional earnings associated with more education) are falling.

Before they can decide how to respond, policy makers need to understand the underlying causes of declining gains from education and training. One possibility is that falling premiums are simply the result of an expanded relative supply of better-educated workers, which would reduce the "rent" element of their remuneration (arising from scarcity). That would be a good thing, helping to loosen labor supply constraints on growth and to increase profitability. It is also possible that the decline in premiums might result, in part, from workers with lower ability reaching higher levels of the education system. Again, this trend should not necessarily be a cause for concern; it is normal that earnings should depend both on ability and on education.

However, the decline in earnings premiums might also reflect erosion in the quality of education and training, an erosion associated with system expansion. If the region's education and training policies are suboptimal, that could result in returns from expanded public and private investment in education that are below their potential level. For example, the rapid creation of new institutions in weak regulatory settings might erode the quality of education by drawing in less able or poorly trained teachers. The system might also have problems adapting to the learning needs of individuals with lower ability endowments and from less privileged backgrounds, whose potential cannot be fully realized with traditional approaches. They might need more support in developing the social competencies and learning habits that can be taken for granted in children from middle-class homes.

Even when specific skill training is delivered with appropriate quality, poor choices of skills could result in a supply-demand mismatch and disappointing returns. There could be overexpansion in the production of traditional qualifications (such as law, economics, accountancy, medicine, and engineering) at the expense of new types of professional skills needed to meet the demands of the 21st-century labor market. Traditional faculties might fail to produce generic skills (such as information technology skills or high-level analytical and organizational leadership skills) that cut across traditional categories and are not adequately developed in existing curricula. At the other end of the scale, low achievers may not get a chance to acquire social literacy skills that would help them learn more and be more employable. These are all potential challenges for policy makers.

This report contributes to the debate about what has been happening to the quality of education and returns to education investment in LAC. It summarizes the findings of a study by a multidisciplinary team of education, social protection, and labor market economists that aims to improve our understanding the links from investment in education and training to labor market outcomes and to provide a basis for policy choices that will strengthen future outcomes.

Following this introduction, the report is organized in four main chapters.

Chapter 2: The Decline in Education Earnings Premiums in LAC. This chapter shows that earnings premiums for tertiary education started to decline over the past decade, reversing a rising trend that characterized the 1990s. This step-shift in earnings premiums is the phenomenon that motivates the study.

The chapter analyzes premiums associated with different amounts, types, and levels of secondary and tertiary education, using evidence from large national cross-sectional household survey datasets. It reports time series for the results of Mincerian earnings regressions for nine countries for the 1990s and 2000s. Unlike most previous studies, the analysis differentiates between secondary and tertiary education. This distinction enhances our understanding of what has happened in the region's labor markets over the past two decades.

A clearly differentiated pattern emerges. For secondary education, in most countries we find a steady secular decline in the wage premium through the 1990s and 2000s. In contrast, the wage premium for tertiary education in most countries in the 1990s tended to increase, but this pattern went into reverse around 2002. There is no evidence that this reversal is due to changes in the gender composition of the workforce or in the sector composition of employment. These trends contrast with those reported in some other regions of the world. A text box summarizes the recent experience of East Asia, where earnings premiums have continued to rise in many countries.

This situation sets up the motivating question for the rest of the report: should we be happy, or concerned, that earnings premiums are declining in LAC? Might it simply mean that LAC's education and training systems are finally catching up with the needs of the labor market, reducing relative scarcity and facilitating a decline in income inequality? Or, on the contrary, might it be telling us that the skills that graduates bring to the market are worth less than those of other regions, dragging LAC backward in the global competitive ranking?

The chapter then discusses approaches to improving estimates of earnings premiums. As is well known, the demand for education is endogenous to ability. In other words, individuals with greater ability are more likely to consume greater amounts of education.[1] This fact makes it hard to arrive at "pure" estimates for the gains from education by looking at cross-sectional data, because the individual's ability is unobserved in most of the available datasets. The result will be a tendency for statistical analysis to overestimate the impact of increased educational attainment on earnings (because some part of the return attributed to education is really a return to the ability of the individual).

We present three approaches to correcting for ability bias in the estimation of earnings premiums in LAC. The first uses family background data on parental education as a control variable, exploiting the fact that many younger workers still live at home, so that household datasets provide this information on their parents. The second uses panel data from Central America to construct individual fixed effects models of the impact of increased education. The third approach analyzes a Mexican household dataset that contains data on ability, educational history, and labor market outcomes. It addresses the problem of measurement error in the ability variable by modeling the underlying ability distribution associated with the observed test results. The conclusions from both these approaches suggest that the returns to education remain clearly positive, even when corrections are made for the ability of the individual. However, the panel analysis from Central America also suggests that the "pure" return to additional education is considerably lower than that reported from standard Mincerian regressions.

Chapter 3: Education and the Demand for Skills. This chapter focuses on the underlying causes of the declining earnings premiums that were documented in chapter 2. Understanding them is critical for determining appropriate policy responses. It first documents the expansion of educational attainment (years of schooling) and then shows how that has played out against the growth of demand for more skilled labor. Economic theory predicts that the interplay of these two forces will determine the trends in relative earnings for different levels of attainment. When the supply of more educated workers runs ahead of demand, the premiums for years of education will decline, and vice versa.

The chapter shows that over the past two decades almost all countries have greatly expanded the proportions of their emerging labor force with secondary and tertiary education, and some, such as Brazil, have registered truly spectacular gains. The chapter then compares the LAC experience on the coverage of education with that of other regions, showing that, notwithstanding the advances, LAC lags most East Asian countries.

Chapter 3 reports the results of an exercise to unravel supply-side and demand-side drivers of earnings premiums. It applies a methodology developed by Katz and Murphy in a seminal 1992 article on the U.S. labor market. The analysis, undertaken for 16 countries, concludes that the reduction in premiums was due to a slowing of demand growth for skilled labor, while the supply of skilled labor has continued growing in a steady fashion. This trend eased the relative shortage of skilled labor, which was previously generating high returns to tertiary education and constraining profitability and growth. Changes within sectors or industries (as opposed to intersectoral shifts in demand) can explain most of the decline in premiums. This explanation would be consistent with a story about a shift away from the pattern of skill-biased technical progress that characterized the 1990s. However, we cannot exclude the possibility that the decline in premiums is related to other factors, such as quality problems in education and training programs (in the broad sense, including both the quality of training and the match between training and the demands of the labor market) or the impact of institutional changes (such as rising minimum wages).

The chapter looks at the role played by minimum wages, arguably the most important labor market institution affecting earnings premiums in LAC. Because they have little impact on the wages of high-paid employees, minimum wages tend to compress the earnings distribution. We conclude that they may have been an important factor in increasing the relative wages of less skilled workers and thus in helping to reduce the premiums for secondary education. If they are carefully set, bearing in mind productivity considerations, minimum wages can help ensure that low-paid employees in the formal sector are not left behind as the economies of LAC grow. Their effect will strengthen as economies become more formalized. However, some low-paid workers may lose out, because higher minimum wages have negative effects on employment in the formal sector and increase informality.

Chapter 4: Education Quality and Student Achievement. If rapid educational expansion were to erode learning achievement, that could increase the likelihood that earnings premiums would decline. Expanding the coverage of secondary education inevitably implies increasing the proportion of children from less advantaged backgrounds, which might undermine learning outcomes. This chapter looks at the available evidence and finds no sign of erosion in learning achievement in LAC during the rapid expansion of the past two decades. However, plenty of evidence is found of large achievement gaps, compared with the Organisation for Economic Co-operation and Development (OECD) countries, and of significant challenges in improving quality.

Chapter 4 presents data from the OECD's Program for International Student Assessment (PISA) evaluation on the learning achievement of the emerging cohort. This test is given to 15-year-olds who are in school. It was applied most recently in 2009, with the participation of nine LAC countries, and the data became available at the end of 2010. The PISA scores show that in LAC expansion has not undermined average learning achievement. Consistent with that finding, there is also positive news about the education of children from poorer socioeconomic backgrounds. In several countries (including Brazil, Chile, and Mexico), the educational attainment (years of schooling) of children from low-income families has improved relative to that of children from higher-income families.

However, there are still big challenges ahead. Recent advances in learning achievement (test scores) are mainly due to improving grade-age correspondence (getting more 15-year-olds into the right class for their age). But the average learning achievement of those who were already in the right grade is hardly improving at all. Most important, the gap in PISA scores between most LAC countries and the OECD remains very big: equal to the outcome of about two years' schooling. Correcting the below-par performance of basic and secondary education programs that produces this gap is a credible policy opportunity to greatly enhance the region's productive potential.

The chapter presents benchmarking evidence on the ratio between resource assignments in secondary education and PISA scores in LAC, compared to scores of other PISA participants in the OECD. It shows that most countries in LAC for which we have data exhibit both relatively low per-student investment in secondary education and deficient productivity in turning that investment into learning achievements (as reflected in PISA scores). This finding is suggestive of a classic "low quality equilibrium," where poor performance makes it hard to justify increased funding and the system remains mired in mediocrity.

The chapter presents indirect evidence suggesting that expansion has not eroded quality in university education. There is no standardized test score such as PISA that allows us to directly track the learning achievement of university graduates consistently through time. However, if the expansion of the system were generating quality problems, this fact would likely be reflected in a growing variance in returns to university education, since weaker graduates would command lower salaries (compared to those with higher ability or those who attend better-quality schools). Our analysis finds no evidence of growing variance in university graduate earnings, which reinforces the findings that education quality appears to have remained stable as the system has expanded.

Chapter 5: Is Labor Demand in LAC Accommodating to Inferior Skills? In the absence of evidence that expansion of education is eroding quality, it seems probable that the decline in earnings premiums can be traced back to demand factors, as suggested in chapter 3. But the pattern of labor demand is not necessarily exogenous: it might reflect the accommodation of the market to the types of skills that are offered. If so, the slowing of demand for more educated workers might be a response of the economy to the quality of skills. The final chapter of this book raises concerns in that regard.

Chapter 5 shows that in LAC countries for which we have data, the occupational pattern of employment has developed differently from that observed in the United States in the past two decades. There has been a greater expansion in LAC of work with relatively lower skill requirements. The chapter applies a methodology developed by Murnane and Levy (1996) that uses information about the specific skill requirements of different occupations in the United States and the occupational balance of total employment in the LAC countries to impute the trends in overall demand for different types of skills. Murnane and Levy's analysis for the United States showed a marked increase in the effective demand for higher-level analytical and organizational skills. In contrast, our analysis for LAC shows that the main expansion is in jobs that demand traditional cognitive skills, such as those associated with tasks in manufacturing, while the demand for higher-level skills has apparently flatlined. The question remains as to whether this outcome reflects the intrinsic demand characteristics of the region's economies or whether it is simply the result of the supply constraints in the labor force (with investment decisions adapting to the available skill endowment).

The chapter presents evidence that LAC companies inserted into the global economy (as measured by factors such as technology adoption and export activity) are more likely to face problems recruiting the skilled labor they need. Enterprise survey data are analyzed to show that this class of firms takes significantly longer to fill available posts. This finding further supports the hypothesis that the available skill sets might be constraining the region's development in some areas of economic growth potential. The fact that in other regions (such as East Asia) the relative rewards of more educated workers continue to increase, while they are declining in LAC, might be telling us that these formal qualifications entail different skill sets in the two regions. It also suggests the possibility that the reason such tensions are not reflected in earnings premiums might be related to the weak correlation between formal education and the acquisition of skills needed by modern competitive firms.

Chapter 6: Conclusions. This chapter summarizes the conclusions of the book and suggests possible policy implications and an agenda for future research.

Note

1. This outcome can happen because the individual with greater ability understands his or her own potential and makes rational decisions to enhance it through education investment (as reflected in the standard microeconomic model of optimal education choice). It might also happen because of socioeconomic exclusion. Children from poorer households tend to have lower ability quotients than those from less poor households (which might be due to both genetic and environmental determinants). They are also less likely to have good information about the returns to education and more likely to face capital constraints that would reduce their ability to access education, even if they wanted to do so. The outcome is likely to be a correlation between the dosage of education and the ability of the individual.

References

Katz, Lawrence, and Kevin Murphy. 1992. "Changes in Relative Wages, 1963–87: Supply and Demand Factors." *Quarterly Journal of Economics* 107 (1): 35–78.

Murnane, Richard J., and Frank Levy. 1996. *Teaching the New Basic Skills: Principles for Educating Children to Thrive in a Changing Economy.* Cambridge, MA: The Free Press.

CHAPTER 2

The Decline in Education Earnings Premiums in LAC[1]

In the 1990s, Latin America and the Caribbean (LAC) experienced a decade of rising relative wages for people with tertiary education that was associated with skill-biased technical progress. But somewhere around 2002 the trend was reversed. This chapter documents this important change in LAC's labor markets. The first section presents a detailed analysis of the decline in earnings premiums to around 2008 for nine LAC countries, differentiating levels of education (secondary and tertiary) and (where possible) types of education (academic and technical). A text box highlights contrasting trends in East Asian countries. The second section discusses whether LAC's declining earnings premiums might be attributed to changes in the average ability of graduates, which can arise when an expanding education system draws in less able students. It reports on three approaches to correcting for ability bias. It concludes that on the available evidence, the downward trend in earnings premiums is not likely to be attributed to this factor, but that we need to learn more about the links between ability, education demand, and labor market outcomes.

The Emergence of a Declining Trend in Earnings Premiums

We estimate Mincer-style earnings functions, where the dependent variable is the log of monthly earnings and the independent variables include measures of educational attainment and also include potential experience, gender, region, and (where possible) training. We use data for full-time private sector employees (*asalariados*) in each country.[2] We use two specifications of the education variable(s): (a) years of education completed; and (b) dummy variables for the highest level of education completed: primary complete, secondary technical incomplete, secondary technical complete, secondary academic incomplete, secondary academic complete, nonuniversity tertiary incomplete, nonuniversity tertiary complete, university incomplete, and university complete (university complete includes those with graduate school). Primary incomplete is omitted as a category. Our reported premiums for secondary education (both academic and technical) show the difference between the coefficients on secondary complete and primary complete; and the reported earnings premiums for university (and nonuniversity tertiary) equal the difference between university complete and secondary academic complete.

Estimates of Average Premiums and Dummies by Education Level

Table 2.1 reports estimated earnings premiums for the most recent year available in each country (around 2008). The coefficient measures the average earnings premium for an additional year of education. This value ranges from 7 percent to 12 percent and is statistically significant at the 1 percent level for all countries. Premiums for a university degree are generally higher than those for a secondary degree (academic or technical)—normally at least double. These differences are statistically significant in all countries except Mexico, which is also the only country where the premium for a university education is similar to that for secondary school. Premiums for a secondary degree are higher than for primary education, except in Brazil, where they are not significantly different. In all countries where there are data, the earnings premiums for a technical secondary degree are similar to those for an academic secondary degree.

Earnings premiums for nonuniversity tertiary education are always smaller than for a traditional university education and are generally similar to the premiums for secondary education. In part, this situation reflects the fact that in most countries it takes four to five years to complete a university degree and only two to four years to complete a nonuniversity tertiary degree. Taking this fact into account, the earnings premiums per year of study are similar for nonuniversity tertiary and traditional university degrees (although the per year earnings premiums for university are still slightly larger).[3]

Table 2.1 Estimated Earnings Premiums in Selected LAC Countries, Around 2008

Education Level	Brazil (2008)	Chile (2006)	Colombia (2008)	Costa Rica (2008)	El Salvador (2008)	Mexico (2008)	Nicaragua (2005)	Peru (2008)	Uruguay (2008)
Years of education	0.10	0.12	0.12	0.09	0.08	0.12	0.10	0.11	0.10
Primary complete (vs. primary incomplete)	0.26	0.11	0.21	0.12	0.11	0.19	0.29	0.15	0.20
Secondary technical complete (vs. primary complete)	n.a.	0.39	n.a.	0.43	n.a.	0.69	0.42	n.a.	0.40
Secondary academic complete (vs. primary complete)	0.25	0.32	0.42	0.32	0.38	0.62	0.37	0.26	0.45
Nonuniversity tertiary complete (vs. secondary academic complete)	n.a.	0.44	0.43	0.25	0.42	0.30	0.31	0.37	0.53
University complete (vs. secondary academic complete)	0.92	1.12	1.21	0.71	0.99	0.79	0.77	0.94	1.07

Source: Authors, based on Gindling and others 2011.

Note: Earnings are by full-time private sector employees. Dependent variable is real monthly earnings. The education earnings premium for primary is the difference in the logarithm of monthly earnings between complete primary and incomplete primary education, the education earnings premium for secondary is the difference in the logarithm of monthly earnings between complete secondary academic and complete primary education, and the education earnings premium for university is the difference in the logarithm of monthly earnings between complete university and complete secondary academic education. Regressions control for potential experience, gender, and region. n.a. = not applicable.

Trends in Education Earnings Premiums in the 1990s and 2000s

Figure 2.1 presents the evolution of the average earnings premium per additional year of education, as measured by the coefficient on the years of education variable in the Mincer-style earnings equations. Average years of education increased throughout the 1990s and 2000s in all countries. In the absence of changes in the relative demand for more educated workers, these changes in relative supply might have been expected to lead to declines in the average earnings premium.

However, in the 1990s there is no clear pattern: the earnings premium increased in some countries but fell in others. Then, in the 2000s, a clearer pattern emerges: the earnings premium fell in all countries, except for Colombia and Nicaragua, where we have very few data points.

This pattern suggests that in the 1990s, in some countries, the increase in the supply of skills was already running ahead of increases in demand,

Figure 2.1   Evolution of Education Earnings Premiums, Selected LAC Countries
coefficients on years of education variable from the Mincer-style monthly earnings regressions

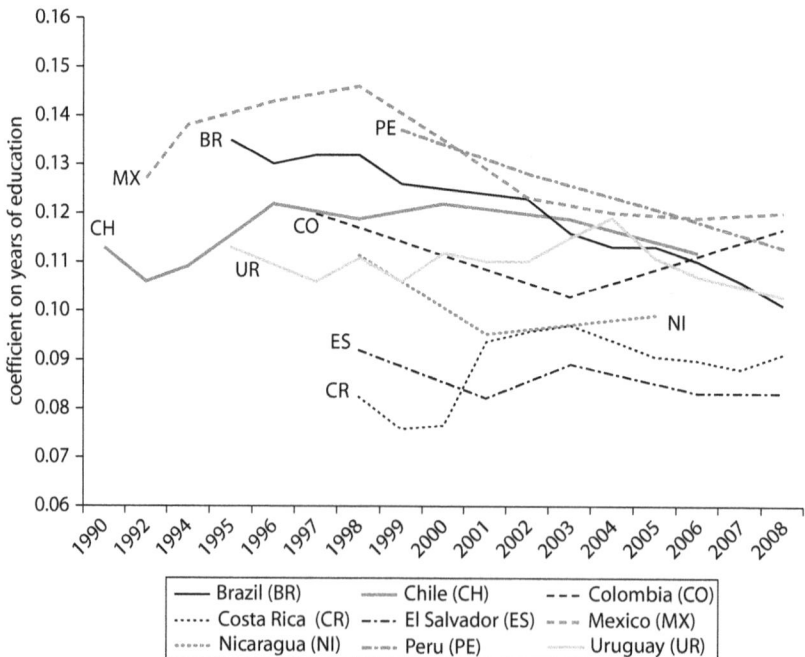

Source: Authors, based on Gindling and others 2011.
Note: Data for full-time private sector employees. OLS = ordinary least squares.

leading to falling education earnings premiums. An example is Brazil. However, in other countries, increases in demand for more skilled workers won out over increases in supply, so education earnings premiums continued to rise (for example, Chile and Costa Rica). But then, in the 2000s, the supply increases won out over demand increases in all countries, driving down the education earnings premium across the region. The patterns suggest that the turning point, where relative demand began to slow or fall in all countries, occurred somewhere around 2003.

Next we examine the patterns of change in education earnings premiums by education level. Figure 2.2 presents the change in the earnings premium for completed primary, academic secondary, and university

Figure 2.2   Evolution of Education Earnings Premiums for Completed Primary, Secondary, and University Education, Selected LAC Countries

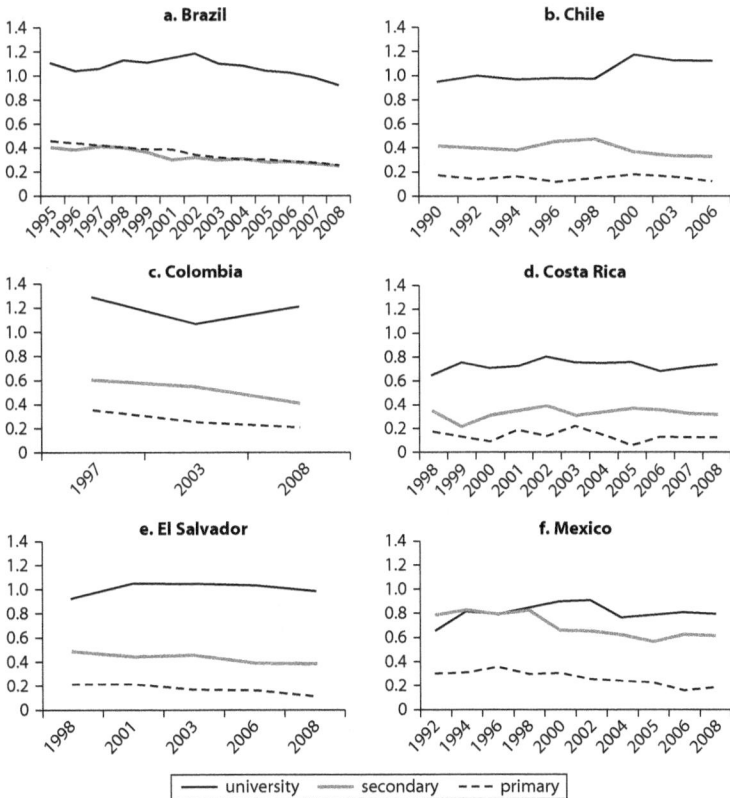

(continued next page)

Figure 2.2   *(continued)*

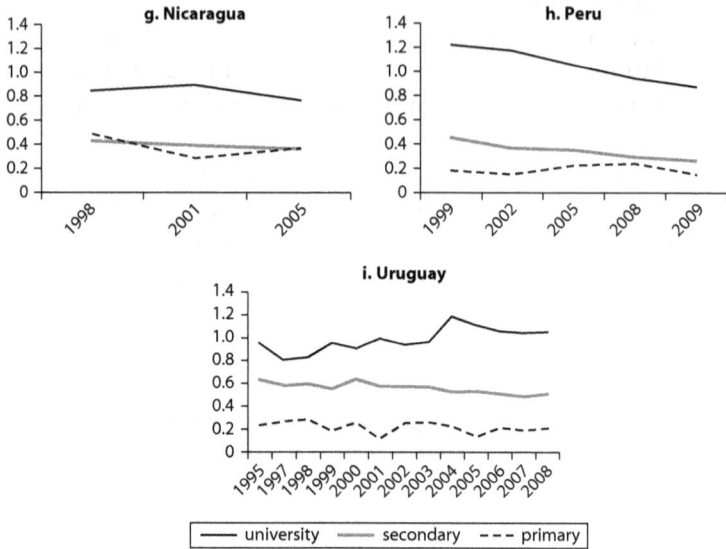

Source: Authors, based on Gindling and others 2011.
Note: The education earnings premium for primary is the difference in the logarithm of monthly earnings between complete primary and incomplete primary education, the education earnings premium for secondary is the difference in the logarithm of monthly earnings between complete secondary academic and complete primary education, and the education earnings premium for university is the difference in the logarithm of monthly earnings between complete university and complete secondary academic education. Mincer-style regressions control for potential experience, gender, and region.

education for each country. There is no common pattern across countries in the trend in premiums for *primary education*. From 1998 to 2008, (a) there is a downward trend in Brazil, Colombia, El Salvador, and Mexico; (b) there is an upward trend in Peru; (c) primary earnings premiums first increase and then decrease in Chile, Nicaragua, and Uruguay; and (d) they first fall, then rise, then fall, then rise again in Costa Rica.

In contrast, there is a common pattern in earnings premiums for *secondary education*, which decreased monotonically in every country for which we have data during the entire period 1998 to 2008.[4] There is also a common pattern across countries in premiums for *university education*. In the 1990s, they increased everywhere except in Colombia and Peru, despite increases in the relative supply of university-educated workers. In the 2000s, they fell everywhere except for Colombia. In most countries, the turning point appears to be around 2003. In summary: premiums for university-trained workers increased in most countries from 1998 to 2003 and then fell in all countries from 2003 to 2008.

We also estimated the evolution of earnings premiums for workers with completed university education compared to the earnings of workers with a completed primary education. The patterns of changes in earnings premiums for university education compared to primary education are similar to those reported in the text. In some countries, we were also able to estimate earnings premiums for technical secondary education (Chile and Uruguay) and nonuniversity tertiary degrees (Chile, Colombia, Peru, and Uruguay). The patterns of change in earnings premiums are the same (in Chile, Colombia, Peru, and Uruguay) whether we look at earnings premiums for university-educated workers or look at earnings premiums for nonuniversity tertiary-educated workers. In Chile, there are no differences in the pattern of change in earnings premiums between secondary academic and secondary technical education. In Uruguay, the patterns of change do differ; whereas the earnings premium for secondary academic education fell after 2000, earnings premiums for secondary technical education increased throughout the 1995–2008 period.[5]

Gender and Sector Composition Effects and Changes in Earnings Premiums

Gender effects. Women make up a growing share of the LAC labor force, especially among workers with higher educational attainment. However, they generally earn less than equally educated men. This fact opens up the possibility that a composition effect might underlie the reduction in tertiary premiums. However, our analysis of the data suggests that it is unlikely that the changing gender composition of employment accounts for the declining earnings premiums reported above.

In almost all countries, the earnings premiums for secondary degrees are similar for men and women, as are the patterns of change over time. Two exceptions are Colombia and El Salvador, where the secondary premium for women starts out below that for men, but by the end of the period it is above that for men (figure 2.3).

Similarly, in most cases, there are no differences between the patterns of change in earnings premiums for university degrees between men and women. The four exceptions are Chile, El Salvador, Mexico, and Nicaragua. In Chile, the earnings premium for university graduates increased faster for women than for men throughout the period. Earnings premiums for university graduates also increased faster for women than

Figure 2.3   Evolution of Education Earnings Premiums for Completed Secondary Education, Selected LAC Countries, by Gender

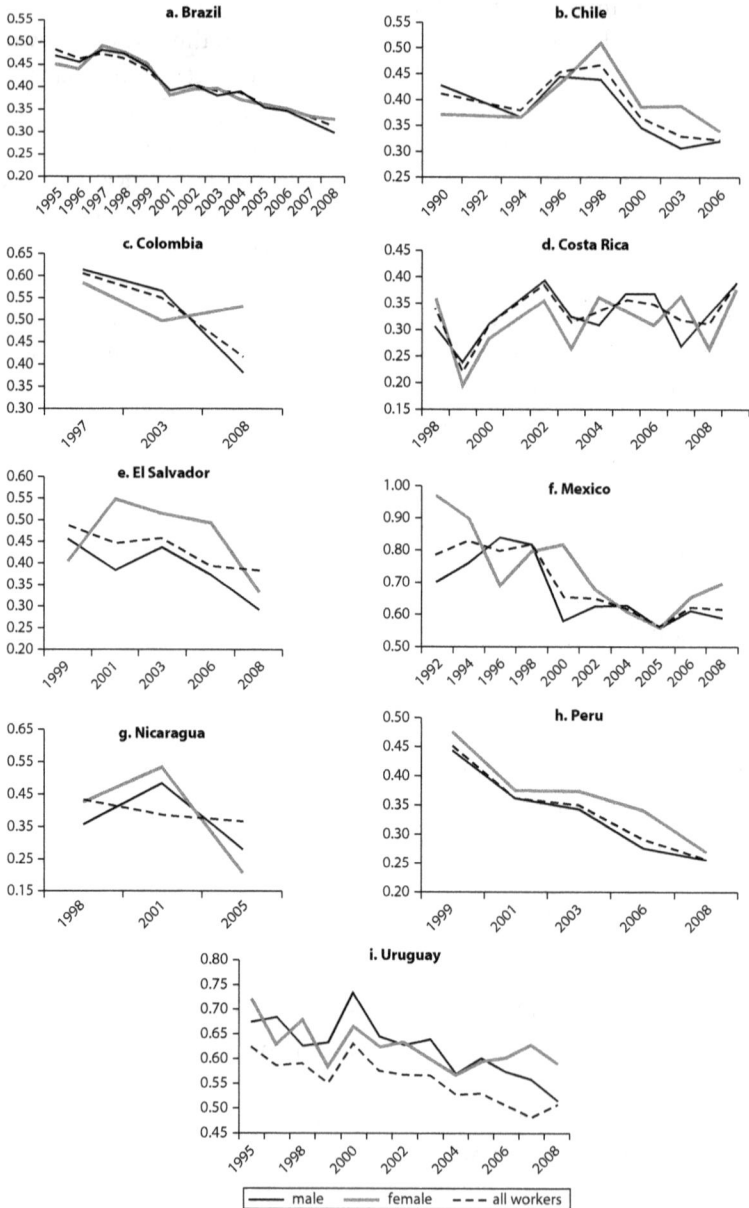

Source: Authors, based on Gindling and others 2011.
Note: OLS = ordinary least squares.

for men in El Salvador from 1999 to 2001. In Nicaragua, earnings premiums for university graduates fell for women but rose for men. In Mexico, the earnings premium for men fell from 1994 through 2008, while the earnings premium for women increased from 1992 to 2002 and then fell from 2002 to 2008 (figure 2.4).

Even so, because women's earnings are generally lower, a compositional shift might have the potential to alter the overall premium for tertiary. This change could happen if the relative shares of better-paid men and less-well-paid women in the tertiary and secondary segments of the market were to shift in opposite directions. But that does not seem to have happened. If an increasing share in the total of less well remunerated women were pulling down the overall earnings premium, the decline in the premium for the total labor force would be greater than that for men alone. But in all countries studied, except Nicaragua, the patterns and magnitudes of changes in university and secondary earnings premiums for all workers is very similar to that for men.

Sector composition effects. The trends in returns to primary and secondary education have been similar across different industrial sectors (manufacturing, agriculture, and other). In most countries, the same is true for tertiary. However, in a minority of countries, such as Brazil, tertiary earnings premiums in agriculture have fallen faster than in other industries.[6]

Controlling for Ability Bias

As is well known, ordinary least squares (OLS) estimates of the returns to education are subject to an omitted variable bias. Ability, an unobservable factor, is likely to be positively correlated with both earnings and education attainment. That is, people with greater ability are more likely *both* to acquire greater amounts of education *and* to achieve higher earnings (because of their ability, irrespective of their education). This fact can bias upward the OLS estimates of returns to education (Card 2001; Harmon and Walker 1995).

An expanding education system in a developing country normally implies the gradual incorporation into education of people with progressively lower ability endowments. This change happens because family backgrounds are important in determining individuals' learning potential and the expansion pulls in people from progressively poorer and less-well-educated households. If so, ceteris paribus, expansion would progressively reduce the ability bias and generate smaller estimates of

Figure 2.4 Evolution of Education Earnings Premiums for Completed University Education, Selected LAC Countries, by Gender

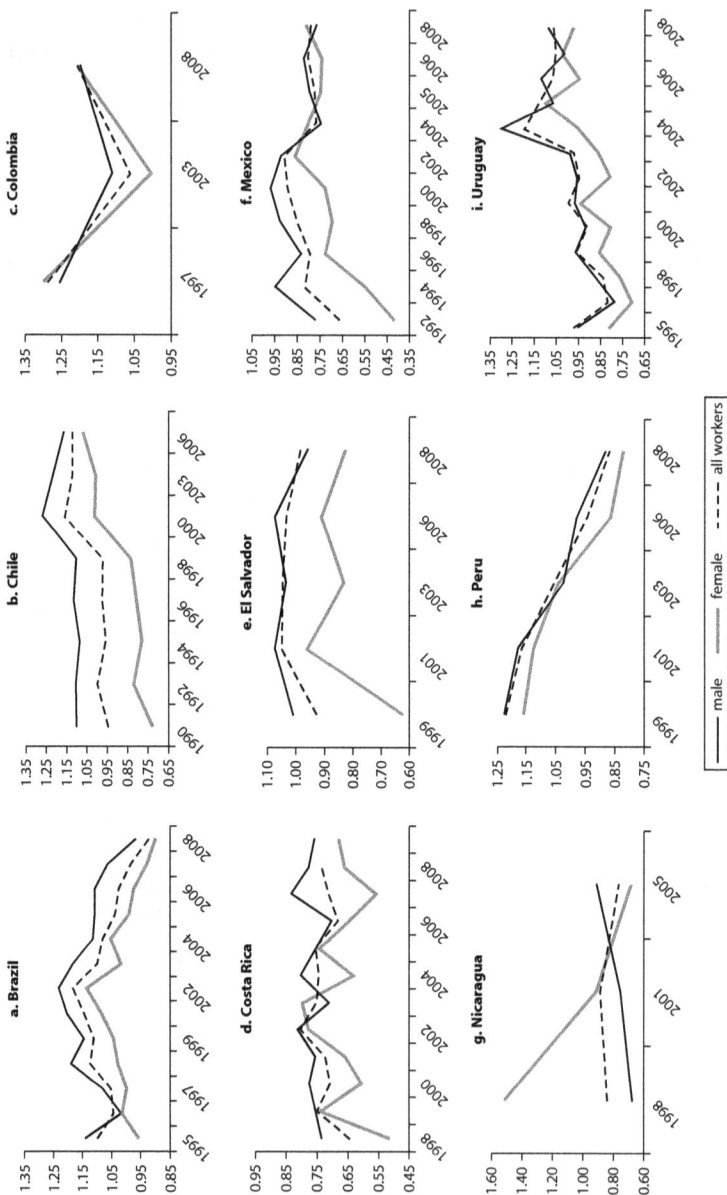

Source: Authors, based on Gindling and others 2011.
Note: Based on Mincer-style regressions.

earnings premiums. Therefore, especially in an expanding system, it is important to control for ability bias.

In this chapter, we present three alternative approaches to this problem. The first uses parental education as a control variable within the cross-sectional datasets that were used earlier. This is an imperfect fix, because it cannot deal with the variance in ability across individuals whose parents have similar educational attainments.

The second approach takes advantage of panel data in the Central American household survey system to construct an individual fixed effects model. The analysis is limited to the (relatively small) proportion of the labor force that reports income data at two points in time and also exhibits an increase in educational exposure between the two observations. This should give a pure measure of the gain from the marginal education. The results suggest that the "real" return to secondary education is apparently only a third of the return that is reported by the simple cross-sectional Mincerian regressions, and the return to university education is even less (about a quarter of the cross-sectional Mincerian estimation). However, we are not able to comment on time trends in ability bias using this method, because we use first differences over time to estimate the Mincer equations, and therefore cannot separately estimate returns for different years.

Another alternative is the use of datasets that include direct measurements of ability as well as data on education histories and labor market outcomes. An example of such a dataset is the Mexican Family Life

---

Box 2.1

Comparing Skill Premiums and Industry-Skill Composition in LAC and East Asia

Di Gropello and Sakellariou (2010) have recently documented the evolution of the industry-skill composition and wage premiums in six East Asian countries: Cambodia, China, Indonesia, the Philippines, Thailand, and Vietnam. These countries exhibit a more heterogeneous evolution of skill premiums than in Latin America and the Caribbean. The more advanced countries (Indonesia, the Philippines, and Thailand) have experienced stagnating returns, while faster-growing but less developed economies (Cambodia, China, and Vietnam) are still experiencing strong increases in skill premiums, despite the significant increase in the shares of skilled workers (box figure B2.1).

Box 2.1 *(continued)*

Box Figure B2.1   Industry-Skill Composition and Wage Premiums in East Asia

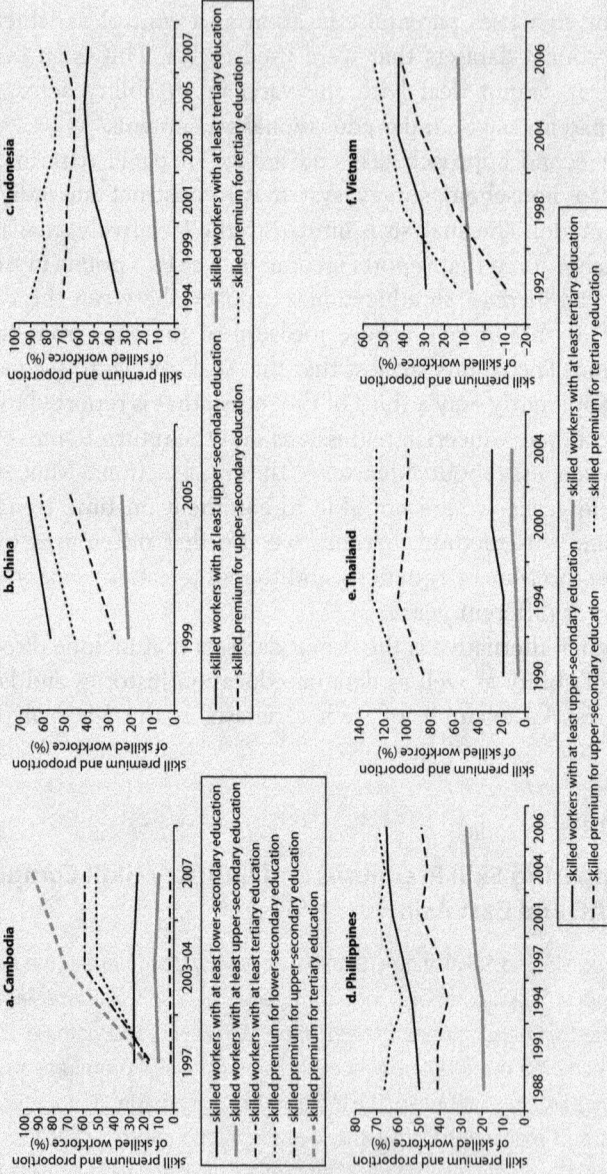

Source: Di Gropello and Sakellariou 2010.

Survey (MxFLS), which measures ability using the Raven progressive matrix test. However, there are still difficulties with using such datasets, because of the problem of disentangling innate ability and educational exposure. It is difficult to get a pure measure of ability in adult populations because having been at school helps one do better on most tests. To overcome this problem, we follow Heckman, Stixrud, and Urzúa's (2006) two-step estimation process, in which an underlying (latent) ability distribution is first estimated based on the observed test scores. The resulting coefficient is fed into an estimation of the respective contributions of ability and education to labor market outcomes. The analysis concludes that ability helps determine education demand and also has a clear independent impact on earnings.[7]

Controlling for Parental Education[8]

One method for addressing ability bias is the use of family background controls. Our household survey data allow us to control for family background for a large subsample of young workers who still live at home and so can observe their parents' educational level. We analyzed data for 15- to 35-year-old children who are employed in the private sector but still live at home with their parents. We reestimated returns to education with earnings regressions that include parents' education as a control variable (the maximum education level of the head of the household). We then contrasted these with the OLS estimates that do not include parents' education (presented in table 2.1) and with another set of estimates including it (table 2.2).

Comparing panels a and b of table 2.2 shows that adding parents' education as an explanatory variable generally reduces the estimated premiums. For university graduates, estimated premiums fall in all countries when parents' education is controlled for. But premiums at all education levels remain large and statistically significant in both specifications, and the differences between the two sets of estimates (panel c) are not very big.[9]

Figure 2.5 presents the time trend of changes in education earnings premiums for university, secondary, and primary graduates from the Mincer-style regressions that control for parents' education. With the exception of Colombia, the patterns illustrated in these graphs are the same as the patterns that we observed in the basic OLS estimates (presented in figure 2.2). Therefore, these data do not suggest that the reduction in education earnings premiums observed since 2002 is likely to be due to a reduced ability bias factor linked to the expansion of education coverage.

Table 2.2 Estimated Mincer Earnings Coefficients Controlling for Parental Education, Selected LAC Countries

real monthly earnings

Education Level	Brazil (2008)	Chile (2006)	Colombia (2008)	Costa Rica (2008)	El Salvador (2008)	Mexico (2008)	Nicaragua (2005)	Peru (2008)	Uruguay (2008)	Mean
a. Mincer return reported in table 2.1										
Years of education	0.10	0.12	0.12	0.09	0.08	0.12	0.10	0.11	0.10	0.10
Primary complete										
(vs. primary incomplete)	0.26	0.11	0.21	0.12	0.11	0.19	0.29	0.15	0.20	0.18
Secondary technical complete										
(vs. primary complete)	n.a.	0.39	n.a.	0.43	n.a.	0.69	0.42	n.a.	0.40	0.47
Secondary academic complete										
(vs. primary complete)	0.25	0.32	0.42	0.32	0.38	0.62	0.37	0.26	0.45	0.38
Nonuniversity tertiary										
(vs. secondary academic complete)	n.a.	0.44	0.43	0.25	0.42	0.30	0.31	0.37	0.53	0.38
University complete										
(vs. secondary academic complete)	0.92	1.12	1.21	0.71	0.99	0.79	0.77	0.94	1.07	0.95
b. Mincer return adjusted by correcting for parental education										
Years of education	0.09	0.10	0.11	0.08	0.08	0.12	0.10	0.10	0.07	0.09
Primary complete										
(vs. primary incomplete)	0.21	0.07	0.16	0.07	0.14	0.21	0.30	0.16	0.18	0.17

Secondary technical complete (vs. primary complete)	n.a.	0.26	n.a.	0.37	n.a.	0.63	0.50	n.a.	0.26	0.40
Secondary academic complete (vs. primary complete)	0.22	0.22	0.54	0.26	0.33	0.55	0.40	0.29	0.28	0.34
Nonuniversity tertiary (vs. secondary academic complete)	n.a.	0.31	0.34	0.36	0.51	0.52	0.31	0.27	0.32	0.37
University complete (vs. secondary academic complete)	0.71	0.93	0.97	0.66	0.78	0.77	0.72	0.78	0.73	0.78

c. Percentage reduction in the premium when correcting for parental education

Years of education	0.10	0.17	0.08	0.11	0.00	0.00	0.00	0.09	0.30	0.09
Primary complete (vs. primary incomplete)	0.19	0.36	0.24	0.42	−0.27	−0.11	−0.03	−0.07	0.10	0.09
Secondary technical complete (vs. primary complete)	n.a.	0.33	n.a.	0.14	n.a.	0.09	−0.19	n.a.	0.35	0.14
Secondary academic complete (vs. primary complete)	0.12	0.31	−0.29	0.19	0.13	0.11	−0.08	−0.12	0.38	0.08
Nonuniversity tertiary (vs. secondary academic complete)	n.a.	0.30	0.21	−0.44	−0.21	−0.73	0.00	0.27	0.40	−0.03
University complete (vs. secondary academic complete)	0.23	0.17	0.20	0.07	0.21	0.03	0.06	0.17	0.32	0.16

Source: Authors, based on Gindling and others 2011.
Note: Data for full-time private sector employees; dependent variable is real monthly earnings. n.a. = not applicable. The education earnings premium for primary education is the difference in the logarithm of monthly earnings between complete primary education and incomplete primary education. The education earnings premium for secondary technical or academic education is the difference in the logarithm of monthly earnings between complete secondary academic or technical education and complete primary education. The education earnings premium for university education is the difference in the logarithm of monthly earnings between complete university education and complete secondary academic education. Regression control for potential experience, gender, and region.

Figure 2.5 Time Trends in Earnings Premium Estimates Including Parents' Education as an Explanatory Variable, Selected LAC Countries

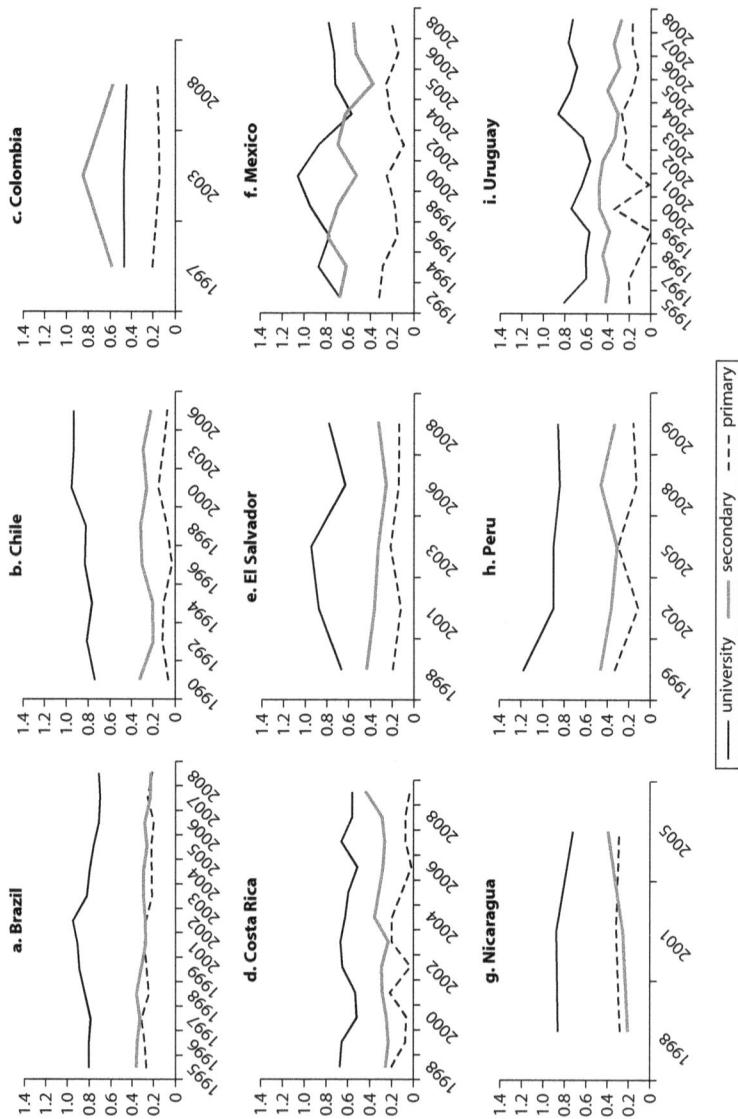

Source: Authors, based on Gindling and others 2011.

Fixed Effects Estimates using Panel Data from Central America[10]

An alternative strategy is to use panel data to solve the endogeneity and ability bias problems. With such data, individual-level fixed effects can be used to control for differences between individuals that do not change over time (such as inherent ability), allowing us to observe a "pure" measure of the effect of increased education. In this section, we present estimates of education earnings premiums controlling for individual-level fixed effects, using three recently developed countrywide panel datasets from Costa Rica, El Salvador, and Nicaragua.

Table 2.3, panel a, presents the fixed effects estimates of earnings premiums using the data from Costa Rica, El Salvador, and Nicaragua.The estimated premiums are much smaller than those obtained from the cross-sectional data. The estimates exclude cases where the reported education level for the same individual falls from one year to the next.[11]

A possible reason for the differences in the OLS and fixed effects estimates is that a different sample is used. The fixed effects sample includes only those observations in which we can observe earnings in two or more

Table 2.3   Estimated Wage Premiums in Costa Rica, El Salvador, and Nicaragua
real monthly earning

Education level	Costa Rica (2001–2007)	El Salvador (2006–2007)	Nicaragua (1998–2006)
a. Controlling for individual fixed effects, excluding observations where reported education level falls			
Years of education	0.02	0.03	0.03
Primary complete vs. primary incomplete	0.02	0.04	0.00
Secondary technical complete vs. primary complete	0.16	n.a.	0.33
Secondary academic complete vs. primary complete	0.05	0.18	0.17
Nonuniversity tertiary vs. secondary academic complete	0.16	0.12	n.a.
University complete vs. secondary academic complete	0.17	0.11	0.25
b. OLS estimates using the sample of only those whose education level changes (pooled over all years), *but not controlling for fixed effects*			
Years of education	0.09	0.08	0.12
Primary complete vs. primary incomplete	n.a.	n.a.	n.a.
Secondary technical complete vs. primary complete	0.31	n.a.	0.69
Secondary academic complete vs. primary complete	0.23	0.14	0.50

(continued next page)

Table 2.3 *(continued)*

Education level	Costa Rica (2001–2007)	El Salvador (2006–2007)	Nicaragua (1998–2006)
Nonuniversity tertiary vs. secondary academic complete	0.42	0.51	n.a.
University complete vs. secondary academic complete	0.44	0.68	0.88

Source: Authors, based on Gindling and others 2011.
Note: Data for full-time private sector employees; dependent variable is real monthly earnings. OLS = ordinary least squares. n.a. = not applicable. The education earnings premium for primary education is the difference in the logarithm of monthly earnings between complete primary education and incomplete primary education. The education earnings premium for secondary technical or academic education is the difference in the logarithm of monthly earnings between complete secondary academic or technical education and complete primary education. The education earnings premium for university education is the difference in the logarithm of monthly earnings between complete university education and complete secondary academic education. Regression control for potential experience, gender, and region.

periods for the same person, while the OLS estimates include anyone who reports earnings and education in any one year. To test the possibility that the different sample is driving the difference between the estimates, we used the fixed effects sample to estimate Mincer-style earnings equations, running the estimates twice: once for the whole sample and then repeating it for only those individuals whose education changed (entered in the fixed effects analysis). These OLS results are reported in panel b of table 2.3. These estimates are similar to those made using the larger cross-sectional datasets (table 2.1). The estimated earnings premiums in panel a are about one-third of the estimates in panel b, which do not correct for individual fixed effects.

We conclude that the differences between the OLS estimates of the education earnings premiums and the fixed effects estimates of the earnings premiums are not due to the different samples used in the two sets of estimates. We conclude from our analysis of the panel data that there is a significant overestimation of OLS education earnings premiums because of unobserved ability bias, but the available panel data do not allow us to reach conclusions about possible time trends.

Modeling Latent Ability to Improve Estimates of Returns to Education[12]

As discussed above, an individual's innate "ability"[13] influences both educational decisions and subsequent labor market performance, which results in an omitted variable problem, leading to overestimation of the impact of schooling on the studied outcome. An alternative potential solution to this problem is to try to measure "ability" directly and include it in the regression. However, this solution raises the problem of finding a valid measure of individuals' ability, independent of the effect of their education. Most measures of ability use tests designed to capture knowledge (for example, reading or math) or more "pure" measures of intelligence (for example, intelligence quotient).

While some of these tests correlate reasonably well with cognitive ability, most measures are usually very noisy and often biased. This is the classical errors-in-variables (CEV) problem, which, in contrast to omitted variables, leads to an attenuation bias in the estimated coefficients of the measures (see, for example, Wooldridge (2002). For example, if higher ability leads both directly to higher wages and to more education (which further increases wages), and a noisy measure of ability is directly used in the regression, then the coefficient for ability will be underestimated and the returns to education will be overestimated. In contrast, if ability is measured after educational decisions are made, then the measures of ability often will be affected by education (that is, they will not be pure measures of ability), leading to biases in the other direction.

In a background paper for this study, we used a model originally developed by Heckman, Stixrud, and Urzúa (2006) and Guzmán and Urzúa (2009) to address these problems. The model relates indirect measures of ability (tests) to an underlying *latent factor* (ability), thus addressing the presence of CEV. Using the covariance structure of the test scores, we estimate the distribution and importance of the latent factor in the indirect ability measures. This estimated distribution is then used to estimate models of educational and labor market outcomes. The model is explained in detail in the annex to this chapter.

We applied this model to data from Mexico using data from the 2002 Mexican Family Life Survey (MxFLS), which included a module to measure labor market performance as well as cognitive ability for all individuals between 13 and 65 years old. This dataset has the advantage of providing measures of ability, education, and labor market outcomes at the individual level, making the estimation much more precise. In contrast, because measures of ability are taken after individuals have finished studying and have entered the labor market, it is possible that these measures captured not only the latent factor but also the compounding effects of education and labor market experience.

Our findings confirm the effects of early cognitive abilities on schooling choices. We find that individuals with higher ability sort themselves into higher schooling levels. We also find that education produces gains in the labor market. More specifically, we find that there are positive, significant, and increasing returns to education, even after we take into account the fact that higher-ability individuals also acquire higher schooling and therefore are also likely to perform better in the labor market.

We find that ability has a positive and significant effect on the probability of being employed for the group 25 to 29 years old, while it has a negative effect for the extended group 15 to 29 years old (table 2.4). This pattern is reasonably explained by the fact that younger high-ability individuals are more likely to study than to enter the labor market. Next, ability has a positive (but not significant) effect on log

Table 2.4   Estimates for the Labor Market Outcomes Model (MxFLS)

Variable	Labor Market Participation		Log-wages	
	Estimated coefficient	Std Er.	Estimated coefficient	Std Er.
a. 25–29 years old				
Male	1.762	0.078	0.096	0.065
Urban	0.310	0.068	0.265	0.058
North	−0.190	0.115	0.433	0.097
Central	−0.102	0.112	0.152	0.096
Experience	0.104	0.149	0.112	0.118
Experience squared	−0.004	0.007	−0.004	0.005
HS graduate	0.222	0.130	0.271	0.102
Some college	−0.102	0.185	0.532	0.163
College graduate	0.835	0.291	1.048	0.224
Intercept	−0.970	0.865	1.425	0.686
Cognitive ability	0.089	0.034	0.048	0.029
b. 15–29 years old				
Male	1.108	0.033	0.089	0.039
Urban	0.140	0.033	0.219	0.037
North	0.034	0.055	0.442	0.069
Central	0.165	0.054	0.134	0.068
Experience	0.256	0.013	0.060	0.018
Experience squared	−0.013	0.001	−0.002	0.001
HS graduate	0.264	0.056	0.215	0.060
Some college	−0.042	0.063	0.364	0.118
College graduate	1.013	0.107	0.833	0.100
Intercept	−1.456	0.062	1.848	0.009
Cognitive ability	−0.027	0.016	0.066	0.019

Source: Authors, based on Oviedo and Veramendi 2011.
Note: HS = high school; Std Er. = standard error.

wages for the 25 to 29 group, but the effect is larger and highly significant for the 15- to 29-year-old group.

The impact of schooling can be seen from the coefficients of the three schooling dummies. As expected, we find that high school graduates and college graduates are more likely to be employed and also earn more than high school dropouts (the comparator). For those with some college, we do not find a higher probability of being employed (which reflects the fact that they are still taking classes), but once again, they earn more than high school dropouts.

Like the fixed effects analysis presented above, these findings are for a single period, and they are limited to Mexico, so they cannot help to determine whether recent trends in education earnings premiums in LAC may be related to shifts in the ability composition of the labor force. But they do serve to underline the importance of ability in educational choice, as well as the potential for improving our understanding of the returns to education by developing datasets with independent measures of ability, attainment, learning achievement, and earnings. In phase 2 of this study, as part of the World Bank's global Stepping Up Skills for More Jobs and Higher Productivity (STEP) survey, labor force surveys in Bolivia, Colombia, and El Salvador will collect and analyze such data.

Annex: Modeling Factor Endowments and Educational Choice

The concept of "factors," widely used in the psychology literature, has been lately adopted by economists with the goal of understanding how to capture the role of innate ability in individuals' decisions and behaviors in life; see Borghans and others (2008). A latent "factor" or "trait" is a feature of the individual that enables him or her to perform a particular task T, for instance, a test (but could be other types of outputs). Many factors are required in the production of task T; here we only consider a factor we call "ability," which combines innate cognitive and personality components with early childhood parental investment (thus a combination of "hard" and "soft" skills). We denote this "ability" factor endowment by θ_i for agent i. Given their innate factor endowment, individuals make schooling decisions in a sequential manner. Following Cameron and Heckman (2001), each agent i makes sequential schooling decisions facing a set of choices given by the agent's prior schooling history, as described in figure 2A.1.

Figure 2A.1   Sequential Model for Schooling Decisions

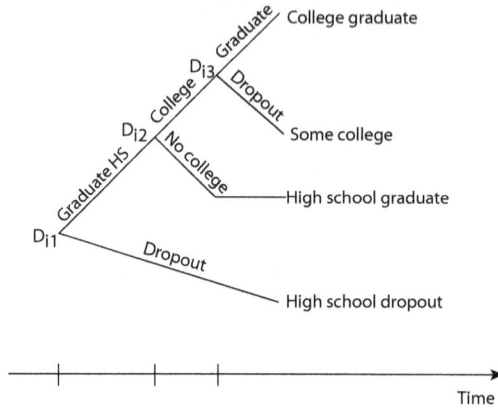

Source: Authors, based on Oviedo and Veramendi 2011.

We model the conditional schooling choice using a latent index structure. Let the reward (psychic and monetary) to agent i from making educational choice j be represented by the latent utility

$$I_{ij} = X'_{ij}\beta^s_j + \alpha^s_j\theta_i - v_{ij}$$

where X_{ij} is a vector of the observed constraint and expectation variables relevant to schooling decision j and θ_i are the latent endowments, which are mean-zero random variables. The latent factors θ_i are unobserved to the econometrician but are known to the agent. v_{ij} represents an idiosyncratic error term such that $v_{ij} \perp (X_{ij}, \theta_i)$ and is independent across agents. v_{ij} is assumed to have a mean-zero unit variance normal distribution. We can define the binary outcome variable, D_{ij}:

$$D_{ij} = \begin{cases} 1 & \text{if } I_{ij} \geq 0 \\ 0 & \text{otherwise} \end{cases}$$

These assumptions allow us to write the probability of making choice j as a Probit model. Conditioning on θ,

$$\Pr(D_{ij} = 1 | X_{ij}, q, D^{j-1}_i) = \Pr(I_{ij} \geq 0 | X_{i,j}, q, D^{j-1}_i)$$

$$= \Phi\left(X'_{ij}b^s_j + \alpha^s_j q_i\right)$$

where D^{j-1}_i are the past decisions taken by agent i. Hence, we can write the probability of any sequence of life cycle schooling histories, D_i, given the observed variables and θ, as

$$\prod_{j \in C_i} \left[\Pr(D_{ij} = 1 | X_{ij}, \theta_i, D_i^{j-1}) \right]^{D_{ij}} \left[\Pr(D_{ij} = 0 | X_{i,j}, \theta_i, D_i^{j-1}) \right]^{1-D_{ij}}$$

where C_i is the set of decision nodes that individual i has visited. Finally, let F_{is} be an indicator variable for agents with final schooling s. So, for example, F_{i4} is the indicator variable for a college graduate:

$$F_{i4} = \begin{cases} 1 & \text{if } D_{i1} = D_{i2} = D_{i3} = 1 \\ 0 & \text{otherwise} \end{cases}$$

Labor Market Outcomes

We allow for the possibility of a causal effect of education on labor market performance, in addition to the sorting effect that arises if education is used to distinguish between high-ability and low-ability individuals. The causal impact can arise when there are separate labor markets for different education levels (so that education levels are priced differently in each market), or when education provides particular experiences and information that affect preferences and behavior (in other words, it improves the quality of the labor supply). Let s be the schooling level attained by individual i, and let k denote the outcome in the labor market.

Continuous outcomes. For continuous outcomes, such as wages and hours, we take a linear-in-the-parameters specification:

$$Y_{ik} = X'_{ik} \beta_k^Y + \sum_{s=1}^{S} \lambda_{sk}^Y F_{is} + \alpha_k^Y \theta_i + v_{ik}$$

Again, X_{ik} is the vector of observed controls relevant for outcome k and θ_i is the latent factor for individual i. v_{ik} represents an idiosyncratic error term such that $v_{ik} \perp (X_{ik}, \theta_i)$. v_{ik} is assumed to have a mean-zero normal distribution.

Discrete outcomes. We model binary outcomes, such as being employed, using a latent index structure, as in the educational choice model. Let V_{ij} denote the latent utility associated with outcome j. The latent utility is given by a linear-in-the-parameters specification:

$$V_{ij} = X'_{is} \beta_j^B + \sum_{s=1}^{S} \lambda_{sj}^B F_i + \alpha_j^B \theta_i + v_{ij}$$

where X_{ij}, θ_i, and v_{ij} have analogous definitions to the continuous outcome case. Since V_{ij} is unobserved, we assume that v_{ij} has a mean-zero unit variance normal distribution in order to identify the model parameters.

We can define a binary outcome variable, B_{ij}:

$$B_{ij} = \begin{cases} 1 & \text{if } V_{ij} \geq 0 \\ 0 & \text{otherwise} \end{cases}$$

Estimation

First, we assume that the factor endowment θ_i can be described by a mixture of bivariate Normal distributions, which is less restrictive than imposing a strictly Normal distribution. The factor endowment is then identified by using the covariance structure of the different tests. We posit a linear measurement system to identify the cognitive measure from the set of tests (T_{ij}):

$$T_{ij} = X'_{ij}\beta_j^T + \alpha_j^T\theta_i + e_{ij}$$

In our first example, we use the 12 questions of the Raven's progressive matrix test administered by MxFLS; in the second exercise, we use three test scores from the Program for International Student Assessment test.

Results

The estimation of educational choices and labor market outcomes is then done in two stages. The factor endowment and school choice can be estimated in the first stage, and labor market outcomes can be estimated in the second stage using the estimates from the first stage. This operation is feasible because we assume the factor endowment is the only element that provides correlations across outcomes (conditional on X_i) and the identification of the factor comes strictly from the tests and the schooling trajectory.

Notes

1. This section is based on Gindling and others (2011).
2. In Chile, we could not separate private and public in all years, so the results include both types of employees. We also estimated the regressions using hourly wages as the dependent variable; using all (full-time and part-time) private sector employees; and using other specifications. We observe the same patterns in the alternative specifications.
3. Specifically, assuming that it takes two years to complete a nonuniversity tertiary degree and four years to complete a university degree, per year premiums for nonuniversity tertiary vs. university are 22 percent (nonuniversity)

vs. 28 percent (university) in Chile; 22 percent (nonuniversity) vs. 30 percent (university) in Colombia; 13 percent (nonuniversity) vs. 18 percent (university) in Costa Rica; 21 percent (nonuniversity) vs. 25 percent (university) in El Salvador; 15 percent (nonuniversity) vs. 20 percent (university) in Mexico; 16 percent (nonuniversity) vs. 19 percent (university) in Nicaragua; 19 percent (nonuniversity) vs. 24 percent (university) in Peru; and 27 percent (nonuniversity) vs. 27 percent (university) in Uruguay.

4. For those countries for which we have results prior to 1998—Brazil, Chile, Mexico, and Uruguay—earnings premiums for secondary education also decreased in every country except Chile.

5. Box 2.1 compares skill premiums and industry-skill composition in LAC and Asia.

6. The data on sector-level trends in earnings premiums are not presented here for space reasons. They are available on request from the authors. The relationship of sector composition of employment to earnings premiums is further discussed in chapter 3.

7. We return to the issue of correcting for ability bias, using other methodological approaches, in the next two sections.

8. This section is based on Gindling and others (2011).

9. The estimates presented in panels a and b in table 2.2 use different samples: panel a is estimated using all full-time private sector employees while panel b is estimated using only those who live with their parents. We reestimated this second regression without including parents' education as an explanatory variable. We found that, in most countries, about half of the difference between panels a and b is due to the different samples, and about half is due to controlling for parents' education.

10. This section is based on Gindling and others (2011).

11. In the three countries, 11.0% of the sample in Costa Rica, 2.5% in El Salvador, and 0.3% in Nicaragua reported that their education attainment fell from one year to the next, which is impossible, suggesting measurement error in the survey.

12. This section is based on Oviedo and Veramendi (2011).

13. By "ability" we mean the combination of genetically given cognitive and personality traits (nature), together with parental investment and the surrounding environment (nurture).

References

Borghans, Lex, Angela L. Duckworth, James J. Heckman, and Bas ter Weel. 2008. "The Economics and Psychology of Personality Traits." *Journal of Human Resources* 43 (4): 973–1059.

Cameron, S. V., and J. Heckman. 2001. "The Dynamics of Educational Attainment for Black, Hispanic, and White Males." *Journal of Political Economy* 109 (3): 455–99.

Card, David. 2001. "Estimating the Return to Schooling: Progress on Some Persistent Econometric Problems." *Econometrica* 69:1127–60.

di Gropello, E., and C. Sakellariou. 2010. "Industry and Skill Wage Premiums in East Asia." Policy Research Working Paper Series 5379, World Bank, Washington, DC.

Gindling, Tim H., Camilo Bohórquez, Sergio Rodriguez, and Romero Rocha. 2011. "Report to the World Bank for Background Paper FY10: Trends in Education Quality and Labor Market Returns in Latin America: Evidence from Household Surveys." World Bank, Washington, DC.

Guzman, Julio, and Sergio Urzua. 2009. "Disentangling the Role of Pre-Labor Market Skills and Family Background When Explaining Inequality." Research for Public Policy, Human Development, HD-11-2009, RBLAC–United Nations Development Programme, New York.

Harmon, Colm, and Ian Walker. 1995. "Estimates of the Economic Return to Schooling for the United Kingdom." *The American Economic Review* 85:1278–86.

Heckman, James J., Jora Stixrud, and Sergio Urzúa. 2006. "The Effects of Cognitive and Noncognitive Abilities on Labor Market Outcomes and Social Behavior." Working Paper 12006, National Bureau of Economic Research, Cambridge, MA.

Oviedo, A. M., and G. Veramendi. 2011. "The Returns to Schooling on Labor Market Outcomes in Mexico." Report to the World Bank for Background Paper FY10, World Bank, Washington, DC.

Wooldridge, J. M. 2002. *Econometric Analysis of Cross Section and Panel Data.* Cambridge, MA: MIT Press.

CHAPTER 3

Education and the Demand for Skills

This chapter analyzes the underlying labor supply and demand factors that might explain the changes in skill premiums described in chapter 2. We present new data on how the expansion of education has changed the skill composition of Latin America and the Caribbean (LAC) workforce in the past two decades and how this situation compares with that of other regions of the world. We then present an in-depth analysis of how the interaction between supply and demand for skills has played out in producing the changes in education earnings premiums reported in chapter 2. The final section of this chapter shows that institutional factors (specifically, minimum wages) have also played a part in this process.

Educational Expansion in Latin America[1]

This section documents trends in educational expansion in Latin America in the 1990s and 2000s, using data from cross-sectional household surveys for nine Latin American countries: Brazil, Chile, Colombia, Costa Rica, El Salvador, Mexico, Nicaragua, Peru, and Uruguay.[2] For most of these countries, we present results from 1998 through 2008.

An overview of the transformation of the educational attainment of the emerging labor force is presented in figure 3.1, which graphs the proportion of the 25- to 35-year-old nonstudent population at each education level for all of the years for which we have data. Figure 3.1 simplifies the education structure, combining all those with any university or nonuniversity tertiary education into a single group (which we term "tertiary"). It shows a remarkable expansion in the proportion of the emerging workforce with secondary and tertiary education and a corresponding decline in the proportion with only primary or no education.

Although the starting points, rates of expansion, and distributions of coverage vary from country to country, the overwhelming impression is that of a continent that has advanced a long way toward generalizing secondary education and increasing the proportion of the workforce with tertiary skills well above 10 percent. The expansion has been particularly rapid in Brazil, Chile, Colombia, and Mexico and somewhat slower in Costa Rica, El Salvador, Nicaragua, and Peru; only Uruguay (where coverage is already relatively high) reports a flat trend.

Mean Years of Educational Attainment

Table 3.1 documents changes in the average years of educational attainment in the 15- to 35-year-old population and labor force in Latin America in the late 1990s and 2000s. We focus on this relatively young cohort within the labor force to highlight the effect of recent changes in education and training investment.[3] Between 1998 and 2008, mean years of educational attainment of the 15- to 35-year-old population increased by an average of one year in the countries for which we have data. Mean years of education increased in all countries both in the late 1990s (between 1998 and 2003) and in the 2000s (between 2003 and 2008). The increase was largest in Brazil and Mexico, where the mean educational attainment of the 15- to 35-year-old population increased by 1.9 years (Brazil) and 1.5 years (Mexico) between 1998 and 2008. The smallest increase occurred in Uruguay, where it increased by only 0.3 year between 1998 and 2008 and actually fell between 2003 and 2008. (This change did not happen in any other country in our study.)

University and Nonuniversity Tertiary, Secondary, and Primary Education

At which education levels is the expansion occurring? The structure of educational attainment by level is summarized in table 3.2; and the

Figure 3.1   Percentage of 25- to 35-Year-Old Nonstudents at Various Education Levels, by LAC Country and Year

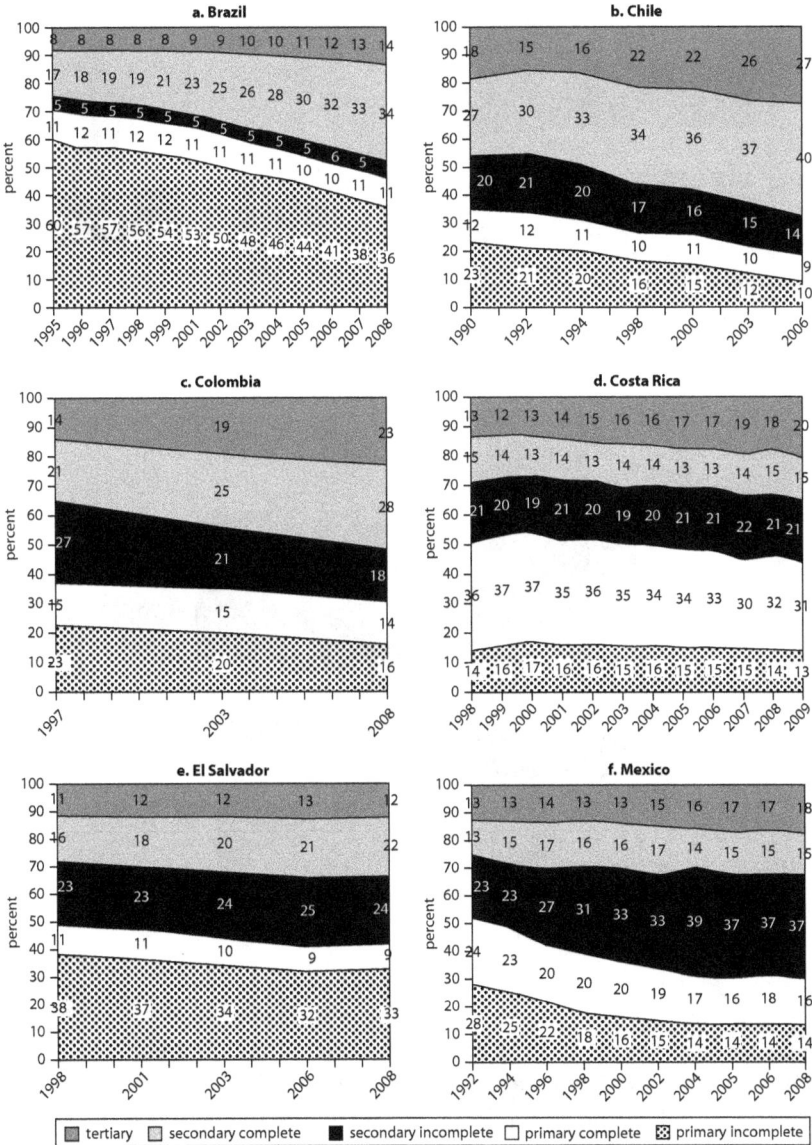

(continued next page)

Figure 3.1 *(continued)*

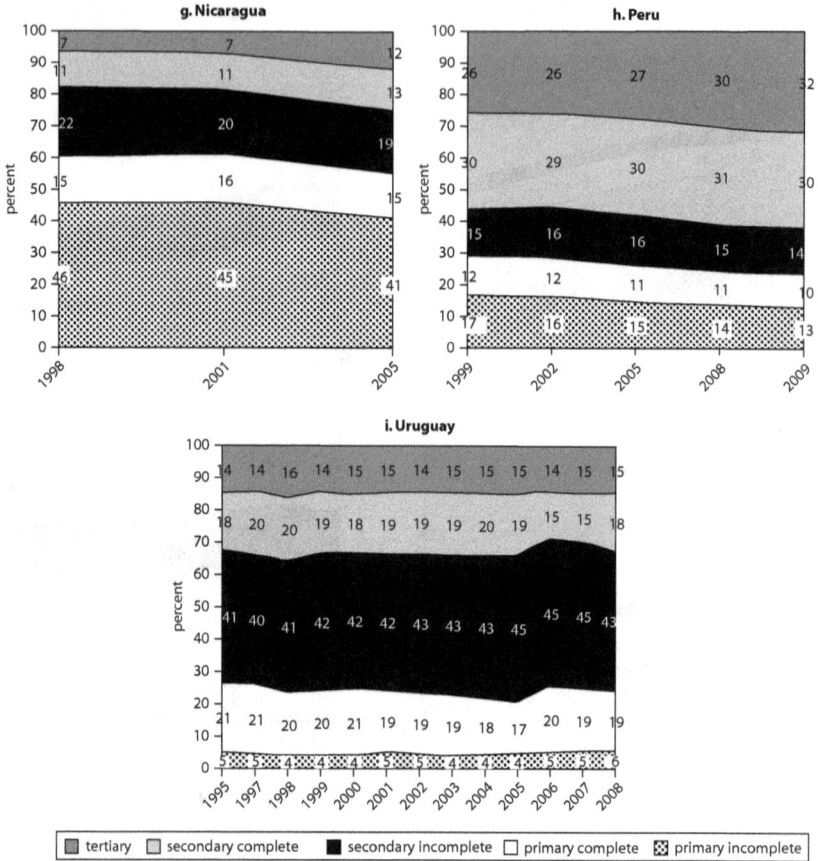

g. Nicaragua

h. Peru

i. Uruguay

☐ tertiary   ☐ secondary complete   ■ secondary incomplete   ☐ primary complete   ⊠ primary incomplete

Source: Authors, based on Gindling and others 2011.
Note: Tertiary includes those with any university or nonuniversity tertiary education (complete or incomplete). Secondary includes both secondary academic and secondary technical. The numbers inside the graphs show the percentage structure for the referenced years.

trends in coverage over the past decade are detailed in figure 3.2. Between 1998 and 2008, there was a steady, secular trend of educational expansion at tertiary and secondary levels, everywhere but Uruguay. We present data on the proportion of the population with complete and incomplete primary, secondary, and tertiary education around 1998, 2003, and 2008. In figure 3.2, university and nonuniversity tertiary complete are combined in a single category for Brazil, Costa Rica, El Salvador, Mexico, and Nicaragua. They are separated for Chile, Colombia, Peru, and Uruguay;

Table 3.1   Mean Years of Education, 15- to 35-Year-Old Population and Labor Force, Selected LAC Countries, 1992, 1998, 2003, and 2008

	1992	1998	2003	2008
a. Population				
Brazil	—	6.8	7.8	8.7
Chile	10.3	10.9	11.1	11.4
Colombia	—	8.6	9.3	9.4
Costa Rica	—	8.1	8.5	8.9
El Salvador	—	7.5	7.9	8.3
Mexico	7.6	8.5	9.2	10.0
Nicaragua	—	6.1	6.4	7.0
Peru	—	9.5	9.5	10.1
Uruguay	—	9.7	9.9	10.0
b. Labor force				
Brazil	—	6.8	8.1	9.1
Chile	10.5	11.2	11.4	12.1
Colombia	—	8.6	9.3	9.4
Costa Rica	—	8.3	8.8	9.3
El Salvador	—	7.7	8.0	8.4
Mexico	7.7	8.5	9.3	10.0
Nicaragua	—	6.1	6.4	7.0
Peru	—	9.5	9.5	10.1
Uruguay	—	9.8	10.2	10.1

Source: Authors, based on Gindling and others 2011.
Note: The years for which data are reported are as near to 1992, 1998, 2003, and 2008 as possible in each country: Brazil (1995, 1998, 2003, 2008), Chile (1992, 1998, 2003, 2006), Colombia (1997, 2003, 2008), Costa Rica (1998, 2003, 2008), El Salvador (1998, 2003, 2008), Mexico (1998, 2002, 2008), Nicaragua (1998, 2001, 2005), Peru (1999, 2002, 2008), El Salvador (1998, 2003, 2008), Uruguay (1998, 2003, 2008).
— = not available.

these are the only countries where coverage of nonuniversity tertiary complete is above 1 percent.

In figure 3.2, the "incomplete" categories combine dropouts with students who are still studying and will eventually complete their degrees. Part of the secular expansion of the proportion with an incomplete university education is the correlate of expanded enrollment and is not necessarily an indicator of growing inefficiency or an increase in university "dropout" rates. To give a clearer picture of the proportion that is completing each level, figure 3.3 excludes those still studying and is limited to those aged 25 to 35; we expect that by 25 years of age most young people will have finished their education. This focus on an older cohort has the disadvantage of reflecting the performance of the education system further in the past, but it gives a clearer idea of trends in dropout rates.

Table 3.2   Percentage of 15- to 35-Year-Old Nonstudent Population at Various Education Levels, Selected LAC Countries, 2008

Education Level	Brazil (2008)	Chile (2006)	Colombia (2008)	Costa Rica (2008)	El Salvador (2008)	Mexico (2008)	Nicaragua (2005)	Peru (2008)	Uruguay (2008)
Primary incomplete	36	9	16	14	32	12	45	12	4
Primary complete	11	9	14	33	10	16	19	11	12
Secondary technical incomplete	—	3	—	1	—	1	1	—	6
Secondary academic incomplete	6	13	22	23	29	42	23	15	43
Secondary technical complete	—	16	—	2	—	3	1	—	7
Secondary academic complete	34	30	31	14	21	13	14	37	5
Nonuniversity tertiary incomplete	—	2	2	0	0	0	0	5	4
University incomplete	2	3	3	3	2	2	2	2	12
Nonuniversity tertiary complete	—	7	7	1	2	0	1	10	3
University complete	12	8	6	9	4	10	6	6	4

Source: Authors, based on Gindling and others 2011.
Note: — = not applicable.

Figure 3.2   Percentage of 15- to 35-Year-Olds at Various Education Levels, Selected LAC Countries, 1998, 2003, and 2008

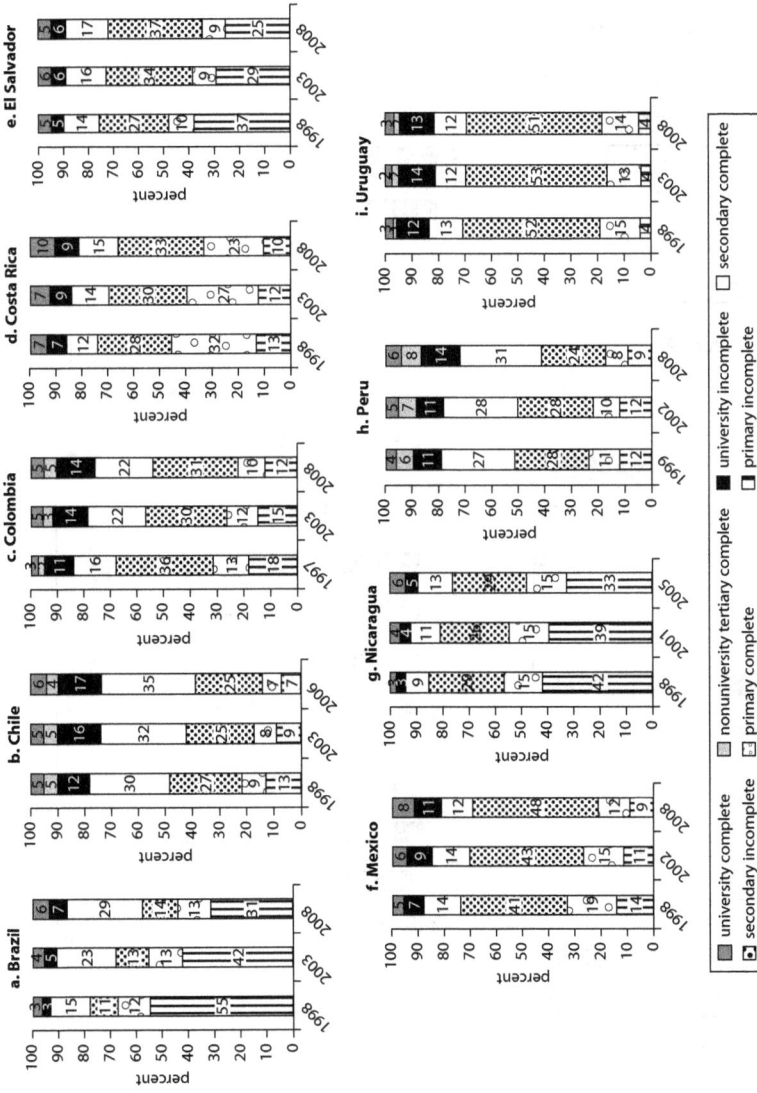

Source: Authors, based on Gindling and others 2011.

Note: For Brazil, Costa Rica, El Salvador, Mexico, and Nicaragua, university complete includes all those with a university complete or nonuniversity tertiary complete education. For Chile, Colombia, Peru, and Uruguay, we separate university complete and nonuniversity tertiary complete. For all panels, university incomplete includes all those with a university incomplete or nonuniversity tertiay incomplete education; secondary complete includes both academic and secondary technical complete, and secondary incomplete includes both academic and secondary technical incomplete. The numbers inside the graphs show the percentage structure for the referenced years.

Figure 3.3 Percentage of 25- to 35-Year-Old Nonstudents at Various Education Levels, Selected LAC Countries, 1998, 2003, and 2008

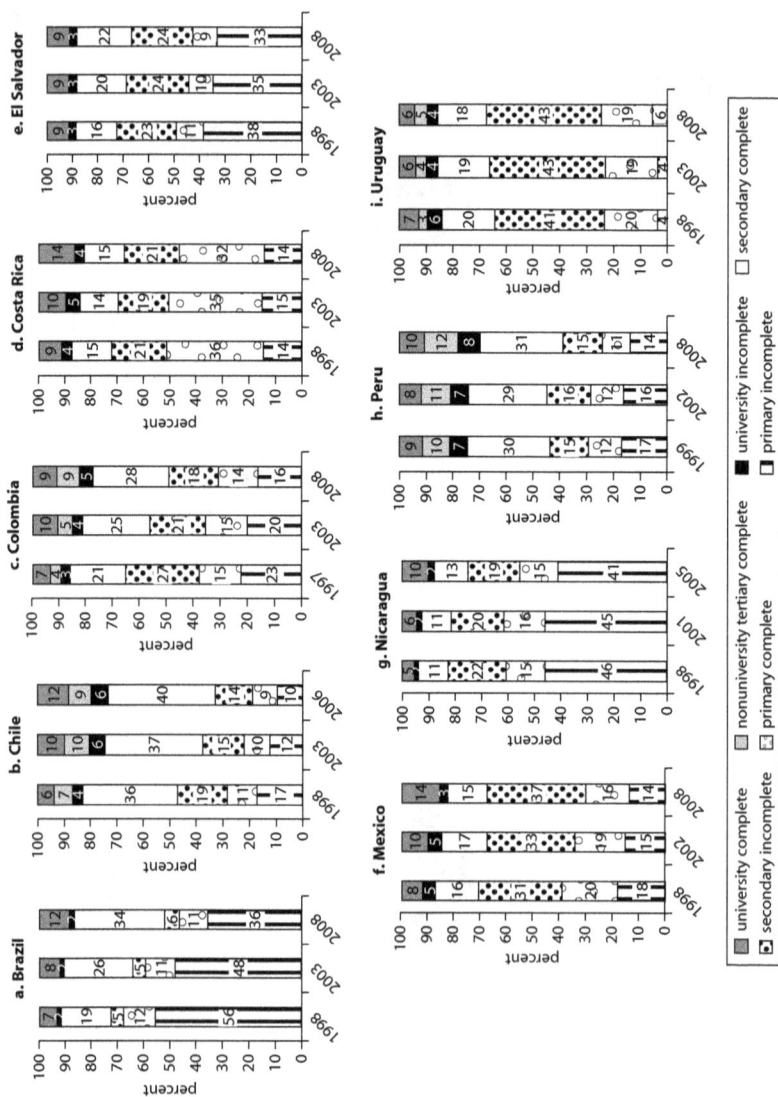

Legend:
- university complete
- secondary incomplete
- nonuniversity tertiary complete
- primary complete
- university incomplete
- primary incomplete
- secondary complete

Source: Authors, based on Gindling and others 2011.

Note: For Brazil, Costa Rica, El Salvador, Mexico, and Nicaragua, university complete includes all those with a university complete or nonuniversity tertiary complete education. For Chile, Colombia, Peru, and Uruguay, we separate university complete and nonuniversity tertiary complete. For all panels, university incomplete includes all those with a university incomplete or nonuniversity tertiary incomplete education; secondary complete includes both academic and secondary technical complete, and secondary incomplete includes both academic and secondary technical incomplete. The numbers inside the graphs show the percentage structure for the referenced years.

Total tertiary (university plus nonuniversity tertiary). There was expansion at the tertiary level (university plus nonuniversity) in all countries between 1998 and 2008. The expansion was small in El Salvador and Uruguay. Elsewhere, the proportion with a tertiary education increased substantially and steadily from 1998 to 2008. Next, we look within tertiary to identify whether educational expansion at the tertiary level is occurring because of the expansion of university or nonuniversity tertiary.

University. Between 1998 and 2008, the proportion of the population with a completed university degree increased substantially in all countries except El Salvador and Uruguay.

Nonuniversity tertiary. Expansion at the nonuniversity tertiary level was an important contributor to educational expansion in Colombia, Peru, and Uruguay, where it grew as fast as, or faster than, the university level. Nonuniversity tertiary is also important in Chile, but there was no expansion between 1998 and 2006. In no other country is nonuniversity tertiary quantitatively important.

Secondary. Between 1998 and 2008, the proportion of the population with a secondary education (complete or incomplete) increased everywhere. The increase in the proportion with a secondary education was largest in Brazil, where the proportion of the 25- to 35-year-old nonstudent population with a secondary education almost doubled from 1995 to 2008 (figure 3.3). Expansion at the secondary level was slowest in Costa Rica, Mexico, and Uruguay.

Everywhere apart from Mexico and Uruguay, the proportion of the nonstudent population with a complete secondary increased from 1998 to 2008 (figure 3.3). In Mexico and Uruguay, the proportion of the nonstudent population with incomplete secondary is high and rising. Close to 50 percent of the population aged 25 to 35 years reports an incomplete secondary education. This statistic suggests that these two countries may have a problem with secondary school dropouts and the associated inefficiencies. In both countries, the first three years of secondary school are compulsory, but not the full six years needed for a complete secondary degree.[4] Many students quit school after completing the first three years and before completing the full six years.

In Uruguay, the decline in the proportion of the population with a secondary complete education masks underlying changes in the type of secondary education. The proportion with a secondary technical education

Figure 3.4   Percentage of 25- to 35-Year-Old Nonstudents at Various Education Levels, Chile and Uruguay

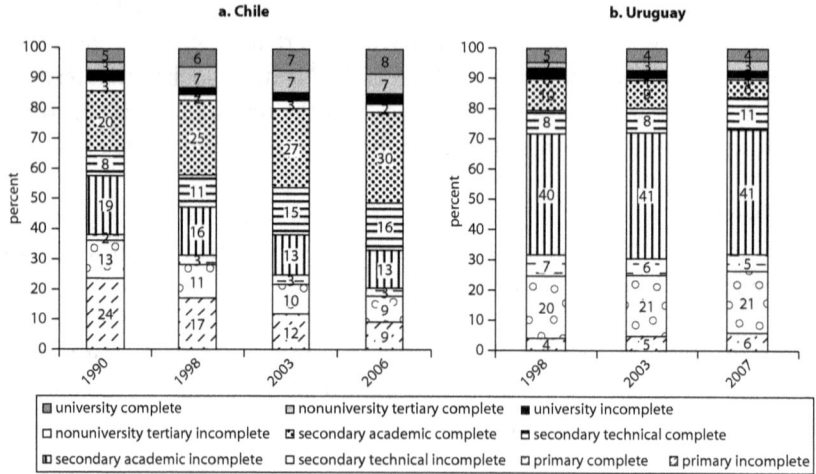

a. Chile   b. Uruguay

legend:
- university complete
- nonuniversity tertiary complete
- university incomplete
- nonuniversity tertiary incomplete
- secondary academic complete
- secondary technical complete
- secondary academic incomplete
- secondary technical incomplete
- primary complete
- primary incomplete

Source: Authors, based on Gindling and others 2011.
Note: The numbers inside the graph show the percentage structure for the referenced years.

increased from 1998 to 2008 while the proportion with a secondary academic education declined (figure 3.4).

Primary. The proportion of the population with only primary education (complete plus incomplete) fell everywhere. Similarly, the proportion of the population with a complete primary education fell in all countries except for Brazil and Nicaragua. Brazil and Nicaragua are the two countries that started (in 1998) with the highest proportion of their population with an incomplete primary education; in those two countries, the increase in the proportion of the population completing primary education represents educational expansion as an increasing percentage of students complete primary school.

Secondary academic vs. secondary technical. In the figures presented so far, we have combined technical secondary with academic secondary to simplify comparisons of the composition of educational expansion across countries because we did not have data on secondary technical for all countries. In this subsection, we separate secondary technical from secondary academic. As noted, table 3.2 presents this detailed educational breakdown for the nonstudent population for 2008.

We do not have data on those with a secondary technical education in Brazil, Colombia, Mexico, or Peru. In Colombia, Mexico, and Peru, these data are lacking because secondary technical education is not offered or it covers a very small percentage of students. In Brazil, in contrast, secondary technical education is important and the lack of data causes problems with interpreting the data.

Only in Chile and Uruguay is secondary technical education quantitatively important; only in those two countries do more than 4 percent of the population have a secondary technical education. Because secondary technical education is quantitatively important in only Chile and Uruguay, in the subsequent analysis we discuss educational expansion in secondary technical education only for those two countries. Figure 3.4 presents the evolution of the proportion of the 25- to 35-year-old population at each education level, distinguishing between technical secondary and academic secondary for Chile and Uruguay.

In both Chile and Uruguay, the growth in secondary technical graduates is an important part of educational expansion at the secondary level. The proportion of the population with a secondary education in Chile increased while the proportion of the population with a secondary education fell in Uruguay. Figure 3.4 allows us to identify how much of the change at the secondary level in these countries is due to the expansion of secondary technical education. In Chile, secondary technical education expanded as rapidly as secondary academic; from 1998 to 2006, both increased by about 3 percent of the population. In Uruguay, the proportion of the population with a secondary technical education increased even as the proportion with a secondary academic education declined. Thus, expansion of secondary technical education is an important contributor to educational expansion in Chile and Uruguay, but not in any other Latin American country that we studied.

Educational Expansion by Gender

Table 3.3 presents the mean years of education for 15- to 35-year-olds by gender. For all years and in every country except for Peru, the mean years of education attained by women is higher than the mean years of education attained by men. In all countries except Uruguay, mean years of educational attainment increase throughout the late 1990s and 2000s for both genders. In Uruguay, mean years of education of educational attainment fall for both genders between 1998 and 2008.

For women (but not for men), more education increases the probability that a person is in the labor force. Therefore, in all countries, the mean

Table 3.3   Mean Years of Education, 15- to 35-Year-Old LAC Population and Labor Force, by Gender

	Population				Labor Force			
	1992	1998	2003	2008	1992	1998	2003	2008
a. Women								
Brazil		7.2	8.1	9.1		7.9	8.9	9.9
Chile	10.3	11.0	11.5	11.7	11.3	11.8	12.4	12.6
Colombia		8.5	9.4	9.4		9.5	10.2	10.2
Costa Rica		8.3	8.7	9.2		9.3	9.7	10.3
El Salvador		7.6	8.0	8.3		7.7	8.0	8.4
Mexico	7.4	8.4	9.1	10.1	8.3	8.8	9.7	10.6
Nicaragua		6.4	7.8	8.6		7.3	7.8	8.6
Peru		9.2	9.3	9.9		9.2	9.3	10.1
Uruguay		10.5	10.2	10.2		10.7	11.1	11.0
b. Men								
Brazil		6.4	7.4	8.3		6.5	7.5	8.5
Chile	10.2	10.8	11.3	11.6	10.0	10.8	11.5	11.8
Colombia		8.1	8.8	8.8		7.9	8.6	8.8
Costa Rica		8.0	8.4	8.7		7.9	8.4	8.8
El Salvador		7.6	8.0	8.3		7.3	7.7	8.1
Mexico	7.8	8.7	9.4	10.0	7.5	8.4	9.1	9.7
Nicaragua		5.8	6.0	6.6		5.5	5.6	6.3
Peru		9.7	9.7	10.3		9.6	9.7	10.4
Uruguay		9.4	9.5	9.3		9.4	9.6	9.4

Source: Authors, based on Gindling and others 2011.
Note: The years for which data are reported are as near to 1992, 1998, 2003, and 2008 as possible in each country: Brazil (1995, 1998, 2003, 2008), Chile (1992, 1998, 2003, 2006), Colombia (1997, 2003, 2008), Costa Rica (1998, 2003, 2008), El Salvador (1998, 2003, 2008), Mexico (1998, 2002, 2008), Nicaragua (1998, 2001, 2005), Peru (1999, 2002, 2008), Uruguay (1998, 2003, 2008).
— = not available.

education level of women in the labor force is higher than the mean education level for women in the population.

Figures 3.5 and 3.6 present the evolution of the proportion of the 15- to 35-year-old population at each education level, separately for men and women. In most years and most countries, the proportion of women with a university degree is either equal to or higher than the proportion of men with a university degree. The largest gap between men and women is in Colombia, where 4 percent of men and 6 percent of women have a university degree. Women are also more likely to have a nonuniversity tertiary degree than are men. For example, in Colombia in 2008, 4 percent of men and 6 percent of women have a nonuniversity tertiary degree. No similar pattern shows up when we compare men and women with a secondary degree—in some countries, men are more likely to have a secondary degree,

Figure 3.5 Percentage of 15- to 35-Year-Old Males at Various Education Levels, Selected LAC Countries, 1998, 2003, and 2008

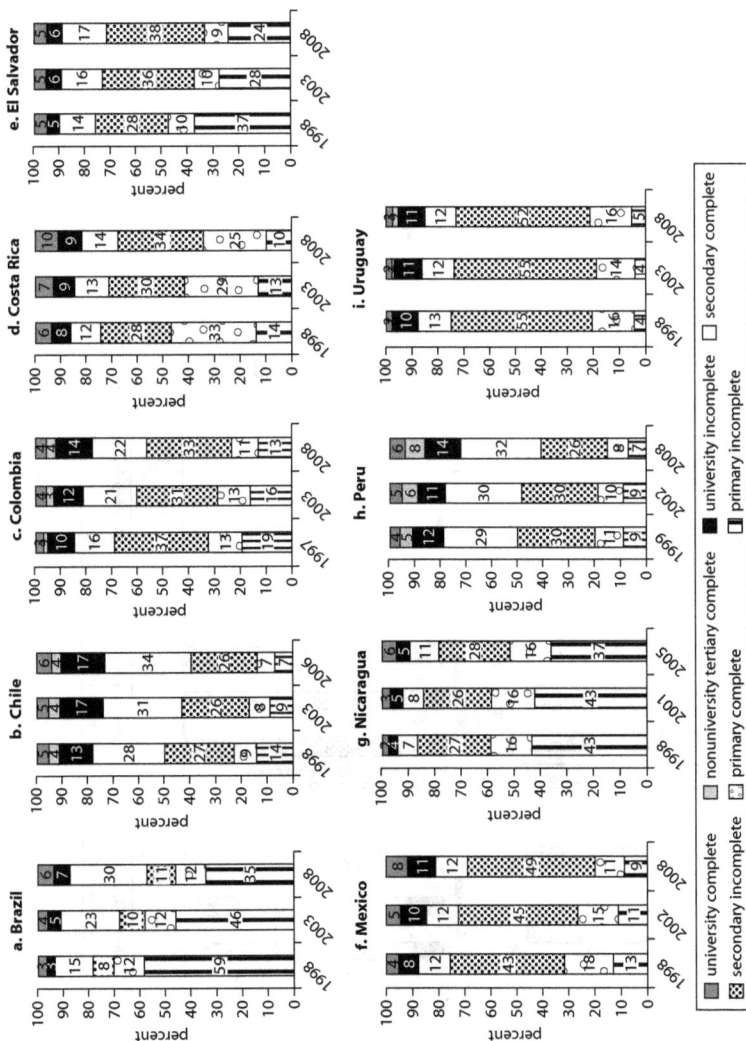

Source: Authors, based on Gindling and others 2011.
Note: The numbers inside the graphs show the percentage structure for the referenced years.

Figure 3.6   Percentage of 15- to 35-Year-Old Females at Various Education Levels, Selected LAC Countries, 1998, 2003, and 2008

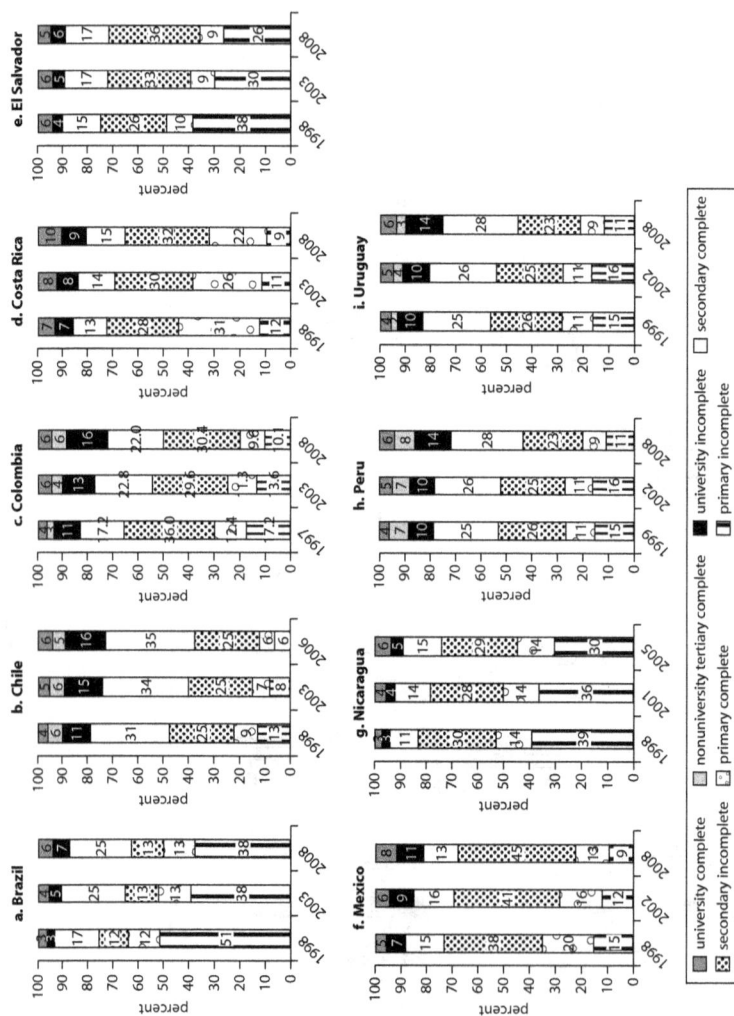

Source: Authors, based on Gindling and others 2011.

Note: The numbers inside the graphs show the percentage structure for the referenced years.

while in other countries women are more likely to have a secondary degree.

In the 1990s and 2000s, the proportion of the population with a complete university education increased at similar rates for both men and women in all countries (except El Salvador). In general, between 1998 and 2008 the proportion of men with a complete secondary education increased faster than the proportion of women with a complete secondary education. This difference may be because women who complete secondary education are more likely than men to continue on to university. For example, in Mexico, the proportion of the population with a complete secondary education rose for men but fell for women. However, the fall in the proportion of the population in Mexico with a complete secondary education occurred because many more women were completing secondary school and going on to the university.

Benchmarking Expansion in East Asia and Eastern Europe[5]

LAC's considerable gains in educational attainment over the past 60 years seem more modest when compared to the accomplishments of other regions. The gain in secondary and tertiary attainment is far greater in East Asia and Eastern Europe (Barro and Lee 2010) (figure 3.7). The "starting point" in 1950 in Eastern Europe was already above Latin America, with "only" 20 percent of the population having no education and 60 percent already with complete primary. Since then, the trend toward secondary completion has been faster, so that about 70 percent of the population had secondary education by 2010, against about 40 percent in LAC. More impressive still are those in the subset of East Asian economies (Hong Kong SAR, China; Indonesia; the Republic of Korea; Malaysia; Singapore; Taiwan, China; Thailand) that in 1950 had roughly half of their populations with no education, but by 2010 succeeded in expanding secondary and tertiary education to reach a greater proportion of the population than LAC.

The strong push in the expansion of coverage of East Asia started in the 1960s, and by 1990 the average educational attainment was already almost one year above the average attainment in LAC. Since 1990, the rate of expansion in East Asia was faster than in LAC, so that by 2010 the gap had widened further, with East Asia reaching on average 9.5 years (equivalent to completed lower secondary), against 8.4 years for Latin America (figure 3.8). In 1950, over half of the population of Malaysia and Singapore had less than a primary education, but this figure was cut to

Figure 3.7   Percentage of Population at Various Education Levels, by Global Region, 1950–2010

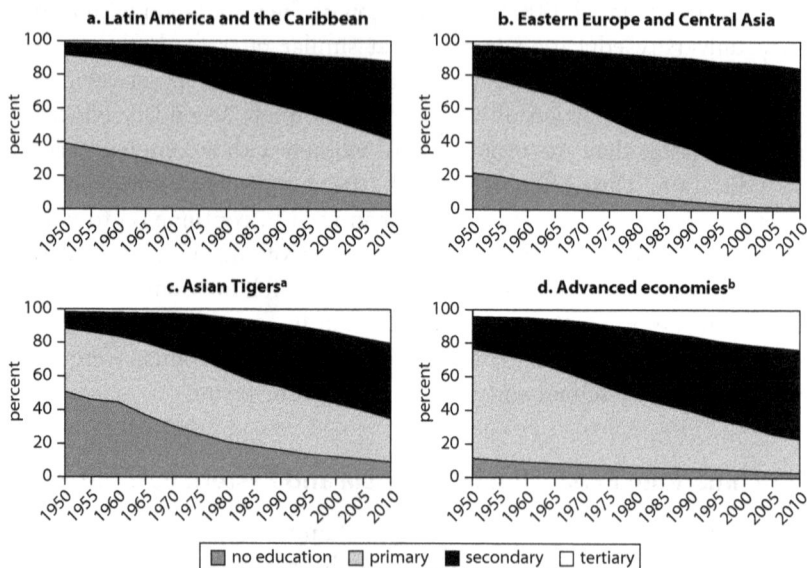

a. Latin America and the Caribbean

b. Eastern Europe and Central Asia

c. Asian Tigers[a]

d. Advanced economies[b]

no education   primary   secondary   tertiary

Source: Barro and Lee 2010.
a. Asian Tigers include Hong Kong SAR, China; Indonesia; Republic of Korea; Malaysia; Singapore; Taiwan, China; and Thailand.
b. Advanced economies = Australia, Austria, Belgium, Canada, Denmark, Finland, France, Germany, Greece, Iceland, Ireland, Italy, Japan, Luxembourg, the Netherlands, New Zealand, Norway, Portugal, Spain, Sweden, Switzerland, Turkey, the United Kingdom, and the United States.

about 30 percent by 1970 and to less than 10 percent by 1990. An exception is Indonesia, which had a fast expansion until the 1980s and then suffered a fallback, from which it recovered only by 2000. The expansion of secondary has been even more aggressive than for primary. By 2010, in every country except Indonesia and Thailand, the largest segment of the population was that with a secondary education (figure 3.9).

Market Drivers of Earnings Premiums[6]

As documented in chapter 2, in most of LAC, the premium for university education fell (or at least stopped rising) from around 2001 to 2003. In this section, we investigate the hypothesis that this change resulted from a shift in the balance between the growth of the relative demand and relative supply for skilled labor.

This section contributes to a growing literature on the roles of supply-side and demand-side drivers of earnings premiums in LAC. It uses an

Figure 3.8   Educational Attainment of Population 15 Years and Older, 1990–2010, by Global Region

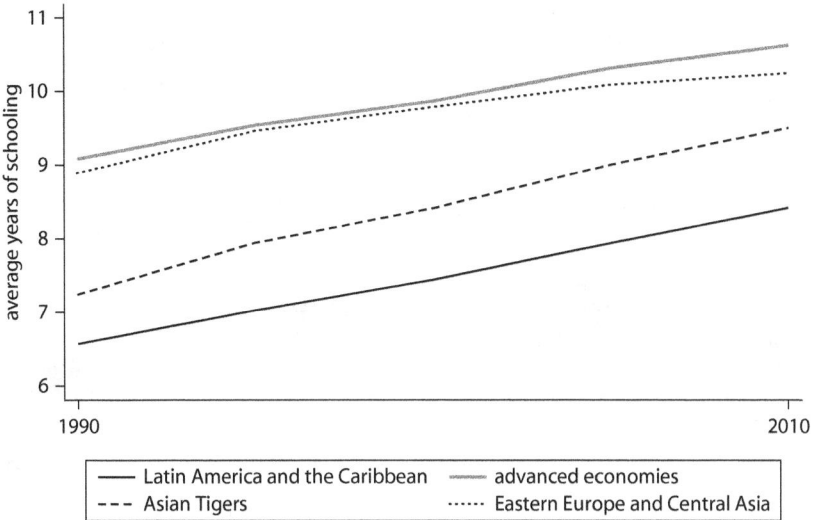

Source: Barro and Lee 2010.
Note: Asian Tigers include Hong Kong SAR, China; Indonesia; Republic of Korea; Malaysia; Singapore; Taiwan, China; and Thailand. Advanced economies = Australia, Austria, Belgium, Canada, Denmark, Finland, France, Germany, Greece, Iceland, Ireland, Italy, Japan, Luxembourg, the Netherlands, New Zealand, Norway, Portugal, Spain, Sweden, Switzerland, Turkey, the United Kingdom, and the United States.

integrated demand-and-supply framework to analyze the main determinants of skill premium evolution in LAC in the 2000s. It follows the influential methodology of Katz and Murphy (1992), as adapted by Goldin and Katz (2007), which uses observed changes in wage premiums (the outcome), together with changes in the supply of different types of labor, to infer what must have happened to the relative demand for different types of labor. The analysis is based on microdata using household surveys for 16 LAC countries representative of 97.5 percent of the population in the region, covering the period 1990–2009 (in some cases, for those years where household survey data are available, we also present results for the 1980s).[7]

Education earnings premiums can be interpreted as the price that employers pay for workers with more education and skills. As with any price, changes in earnings premiums are the result of changes in supply and demand. Increases in the relative supply of more educated workers (brought about by educational expansion) would put pressure on the earnings premiums to fall, while increases in the relative demand for more educated workers would put pressure on the earnings premiums to rise.

Figure 3.9   Percentage of Population 15 Years and Older with Various Levels of Education, Selected East Asian Economies, 1950–2010

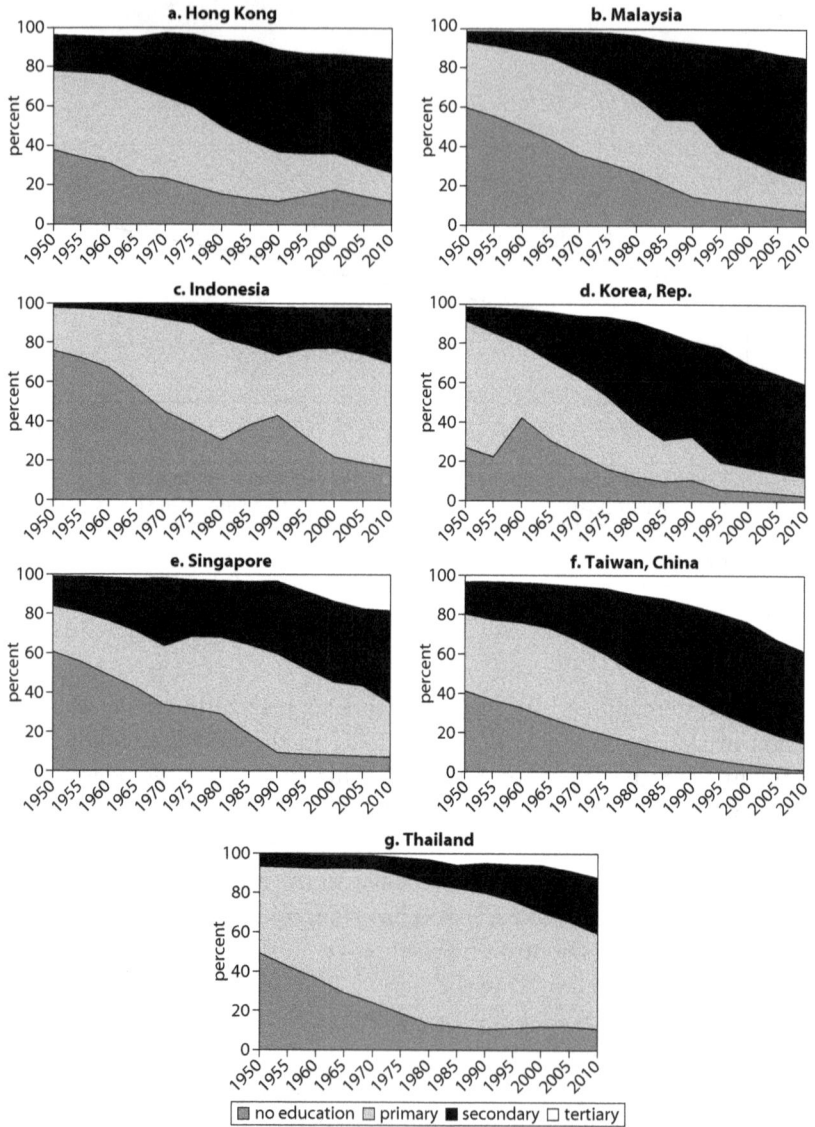

a. Hong Kong

b. Malaysia

c. Indonesia

d. Korea, Rep.

e. Singapore

f. Taiwan, China

g. Thailand

☐ no education ☐ primary ■ secondary ☐ tertiary

Source: Barro and Lee 2010.

In the 1990s, skill shortages seemed to be a binding constraint to growth in the region. Although the average skill level of the workforce was rising in most countries, labor market skill premiums were stable or rising. This fact suggested that the expansion in the supply of skills had lagged behind demand. In this period, the global economy was growing fast, many countries in LAC had growing access to the world market, labor market institutions were becoming more flexible, and the pattern of technological change seemed to be biased toward higher skill levels in the workforce (De Ferranti and others 2003). Evidence for Argentina, Brazil, Chile, Colombia, Costa Rica, and Mexico suggested that trade liberalization and skill-biased technical progress were driving the increased demand for skills (Harrison and Hanson 1999; Robbins and Gindling 1999; Gill and Montenegro 2002; Galiani and Sanguinetti 2003; Attanasio, Golberg, and Pavcnik 2004; Acosta and Gasparini 2007; and Manacorda, Sanchez-Paramo, and Schady 2010).

The fall in skill premiums observed in the 2000s could reflect the impact of the continued expansion of the supply of skilled workers in the face of declining growth in the demand for their skills. As suggested by Goldin and Katz (2007) for the United States and López-Calva and Lustig (2009) for LAC, in Jan Tinbergen's "race between education and technology" education may be pulling ahead.

Declining growth in the demand for skilled labor in LAC could be related to a slowdown in the process of skill-biased technological change or to a shift in the structure of production away from agriculture and manufacturing toward low-skill-intensive sectors such as services (for example, commerce and construction) and the extraction of natural resources. This shift might, in turn, be linked to structural reforms such as trade liberalization and privatization. Other plausible hypotheses include (a) the possibility that the increase in minimum wages and recovery of union power led to a rise in relative wages of low-skilled workers (dealt with in this chapter); and (b) the failure of educational expansion to feed into faster productivity growth (discussed in chapters 4 and 5).

Demand and Supply Factors Underlying Earnings Premiums

Changes in the industry structure of employment, resulting from changes in relative prices and economic policy, may act as a powerful demand shifter in the labor market (Katz and Murphy 1992). This section documents patterns in skill wage premiums and relative labor supply and estimates the relative demands consistent with those patterns. It also carries out decompositions to illustrate the between-sector and within-sector factors underlying changes in employment patterns. The purpose is to determine to what extent changes in relative demand can be explained by changes in the structure of production in LAC, and to what extent they are accounted for by common factors running across industries. We find evidence that the fall in the wage premium for workers with a tertiary education in the 2000s was mostly explained by a fall in the relative demand for workers with a tertiary education, and not only by an increase in the relative supply.

Consistent with the results documented in chapter 1, our analysis confirms that the tertiary skill wage premium widened in the 1990s for most countries in the region (figures 3.10, 3.11, and 3.12).[8] This pattern was widespread across countries, noticeably in Argentina, Bolivia, Colombia, and Nicaragua, but not completely generalized (Brazil is an exception). In the 2000s, in contrast, the tertiary wage premium fell across all the 16 LAC economies. The fall started in the late 1990s in some economies (such as Mexico) and around 2002 to 2003 in South American economies, in the aftermath of serious macroeconomic crises (for example, Brazil in 1998; Argentina, Paraguay, and Uruguay in 2001). The fall in the tertiary wage gap continued throughout the decade, unaffected by the recent economic crisis. In most countries, the fall was big enough to offset the increase in the 1990s, lowering the premium back to levels registered 20 years ago.

The rise in skill premiums and the supply of tertiary workers in the 1990s suggests a strong increase in the relative demand for skilled labor in the 1990s throughout LAC ("technology winning the race over education") (see box 3.1 for the methodology). In contrast, in the 2000s the balance changed. The increase in relative supply of skilled workers cannot by itself explain the decline in skill premiums in the 2000s. The gap between the evolution of relative supply and the skill premiums signals a decline in the relative demand for tertiary educated workers in the 2000s in all but two countries in LAC ("education winning the race over technology").[9]

Sector-Based Demand Shifts

In the previous section, we presented evidence that a supply-side story, alone, cannot explain the evolution in the price of skilled labor over the past two decades in LAC. Demand-side shifters have been operating as well, moving in opposite directions in the 1990s and 2000s. In this section, we carry out decompositions to determine if there is evidence to support the hypothesis that observed changes in relative demand for skilled labor

Figure 3.10 Wage Premium Index and Supply and Demand Indexes, MERCOSUR

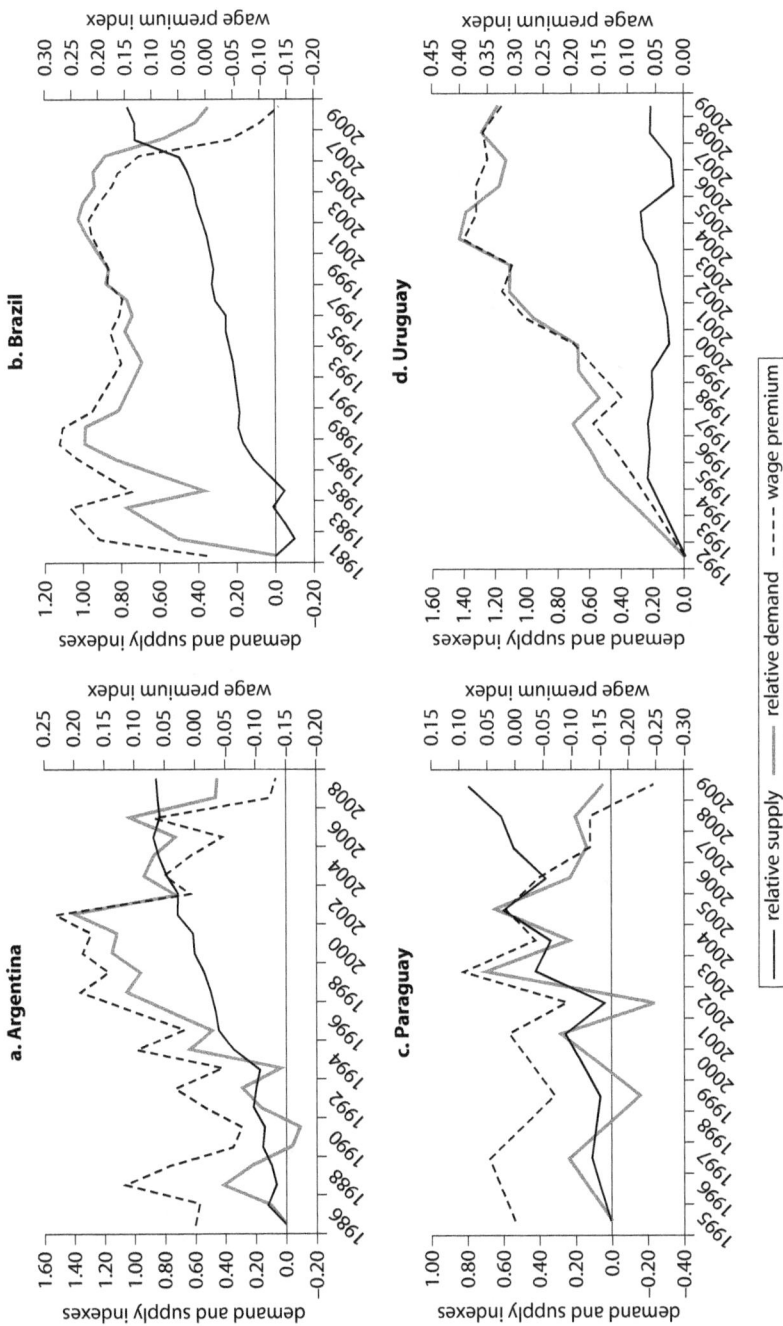

Source: Authors' calculations based on household surveys. Demand computation assumes an elasticity of substitution of 3. Details on sample years, survey, and methodology are available in Acosta and others 2011.

Note: MERCOSUR = Mercado Común del Sur (Southern Common Market).

Figure 3.11 Wage Premium Index and Supply and Demand Indexes, Andean Countries

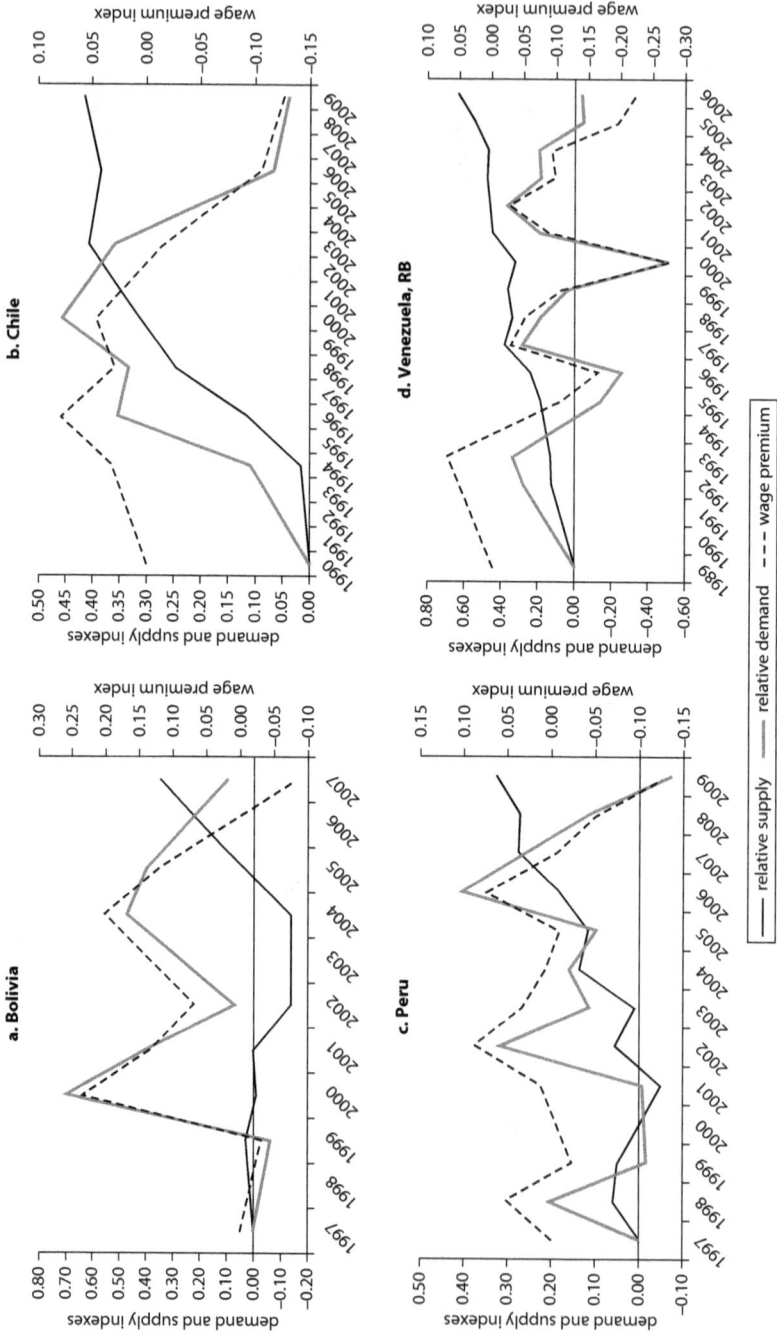

Source: Authors' calculations based on household surveys. Demand computation assumes an elasticity of substitution of 3. Details on sample years, survey, and methodology are available in Acosta and others 2011.

Figure 3.12 Wage Premium Index and Supply and Demand Indexes, Mexico and Central America

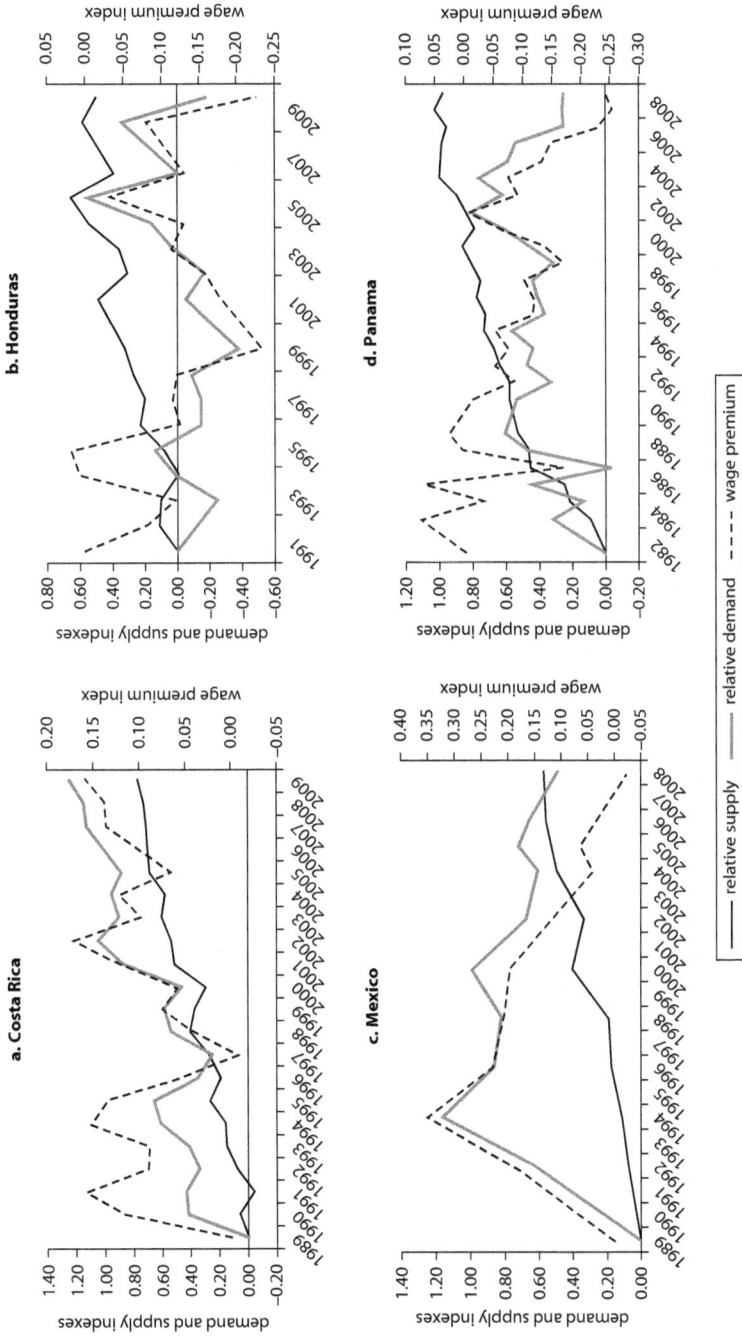

a. Costa Rica

b. Honduras

c. Mexico

d. Panama

— relative supply   —— relative demand   - - - - wage premium

Source: Authors' calculations based on household surveys. Demand computation assumes an elasticity of substitution of 3. Details on sample years, survey, and methodology are available in Acosta and others 2011.

Box 3.1

Supply and Demand Framework for Measuring Determinants of Returns to Skill

The methodology to estimate supply and demand shifters of skill premium evolution follows the work initiated by Katz and Murphy (1992) and the subsequent contributions. The basic framework assumes a constant elasticity of substitution production function with two factors:

$$Q_t = A_t \left[\lambda_t S_t^\rho + (1 - \lambda_t) U_t^\rho \right]^{\frac{1}{\rho}}$$

where Q is output; A is total factor productivity; λ and ρ are technology parameters; and S and U are the two factors that represent units of skilled and unskilled labor, respectively. Within this framework, under perfect competition, the skilled wage premium (w_s/w_u) in year t satisfies the following relationship:

$$\log\left(\frac{W_S(t)}{W_U(t)} \right) = \frac{1}{\sigma} \left[D(t) - \log\left(\frac{S(t)}{U(t)} \right) \right]$$

where σ is the (unknown) elasticity of substitution between the two types of labor, and $D(t)$ is the (unobservable) relative demand for these two factors measured in log quantity units. The greater the elasticity of substitution between the two factors, the greater must be the fluctuations in $D(t)$ to explain any given time series of relative prices, for a given time series of observed relative quantities.

The wage premium (w_s/w_u) is obtained by means of a Mincerian regression of the logarithm of the hourly wage of workers aged 26 to 56 years on a set of controls that includes educational attainment, years of experience, region of residence, and urban or rural status (when available).

To derive the relative supply $S(t)/U(t)$, the population of each country is divided into 24 groups according to their educational level, gender, and potential experience. Then, in each year the average wage for each group is divided by the wage of the largest group. The resulting relative wages constitute the weights used to compute the aggregate supply for each group considered, measured in efficiency units. These efficiency-adjusted labor supplies are then added together for all main educational groups (primary, secondary, tertiary) to get an estimate of the total supply of labor at each education level. To calculate the relative supply of skilled labor in each year and country, $S(t)$ is measured as the total supply of workers with a university education in each year and $U(t)$ is measured as the sum of the total supply of workers with a secondary and primary education in each year.

(continued next page)

Box Table B3.1 Changes in the Wage Premium and the Supply and Demand for Skilled (Tertiary Educated) vs. Unskilled (Other Educational Groups) Workers in LAC

	Wage Premium		Relative Supply		Relative Demand σsu = 2		Relative Demand σsu = 3	
	1990s	2000s	1990s	2000s	1990s	2000s	1990s	2000s
Argentina	3.5	−2.4	4.6	2.4	11.5	−2.3	15.0	−4.7
Bolivia	7.9	−4.6	−0.2	5.1	15.6	−4.1	23.5	−8.7
Brazil	−0.4	−3.2	1.6	4.4	0.8	−1.9	0.4	−5.1
Chile	0.5	−1.9	3.1	1.1	4.1	−2.7	4.6	−4.7
Colombia	2.5	−2.0	6.4	6.0	11.5	2.1	14.0	0.1
Costa Rica	0.4	−0.2	4.0	3.4	4.9	3.0	5.3	2.8
Ecuador	—	−3.2	—	3.4	—	−3.0	—	−6.3
El Salvador	1.7	−0.1	5.5	−0.3	8.9	−0.4	10.6	−0.5
Honduras	0.0	−1.9	2.6	2.3	2.6	−1.4	2.6	−3.3
Mexico	1.8	−2.8	3.6	2.2	7.2	−3.5	9.0	−6.3
Nicaragua	3.5	−6.9	4.6	6.6	11.6	−7.2	15.0	−14.1
Panama	0.3	−2.3	2.3	2.4	2.9	−2.2	3.1	−4.4
Paraguay	0.8	−5.6	5.3	6.1	6.9	−5.2	7.6	−10.8
Peru	0.6	−2.8	0.2	3.8	1.3	−1.8	1.9	−4.6
Uruguay	2.2	−1.3	2.9	−0.8	7.3	−3.5	9.6	−4.8
Venezuela, RB	1.1	−4.8	3.9	4.2	6.2	−5.4	7.3	−10.3
Mean	1.8	−2.9	3.4	3.3	6.9	−2.5	8.6	−5.4

Source: Authors' calculations based on microdata from household surveys. Details on sample years, survey, and methodology are available in Acosta and others 2011.

Note: — = not available. For each country and period, the table shows the percentage change of the wage premium (columns 1 and 2), the relative supply of skilled workers (columns 3 and 4), and the estimated change in the relative demand for skilled workers, consistent with an elasticity of substitution of 2 (columns 5 and 6) and of 3 (columns 7 and 8).

(continued next page)

Box 3.1 *(continued)*

An estimation of σ is needed to implement this methodology. Most of the literature gets that estimation from the inverse of the coefficient of the relative supply of skilled labor in a wage gap regression, controlling by proxies of the relative demand—usually a time trend, linear or of higher order. Using this methodology, Manacorda, Sanchez-Paramo, and Schady (2010) find values around 3 for LAC in the 1990s. Goldin and Katz (2007) in their study for the United States use lower values—around 1.6. Given this broad range of estimations, it was decided to use alternative values of the elasticity of substitution to check for robustness; in table 3.4, we present estimates assuming two values of σ (2 and 3).

Source: Authors.

can be explained by changes in the sector or industry structure of production in LAC, or the alternative hypothesis that it is due to factors that are common across industries.

We find that all countries in the region upgraded the skill content of their labor force in the 1990s and 2000s, but only a small part of that process can be linked to shifts in the sectoral composition of production. In contrast, with some exceptions, within-sector changes were more relevant in both decades, with similar patterns of skill upgrading found across most industries. These "equilibrium effects" arising from demand and supply interactions suggest that the rise and fall in relative demand for skilled labor in the 1990s and 2000s, respectively, arose from factors that were common to all sectors or industries (such as technological change or labor market regulations), and not from a shift in the structure of production (for example, toward more skill-intensive sectors or industries in the 1990s and less skill-intensive sectors or industries in the 2000s).

Box 3.2 describes a decomposition technique that helps us disentangle whether changes in the skill content of employment are driven mainly by changes in the sector composition of production (the "between effect") or by factors internal to economic sectors or industries (the "within effect"). There might be exogenous sources of changes in both between and within factors, but there can also be changes driven by changes in factor prices. Katz and Murphy (1992) and others argue that the "between effect" could reflect changes resulting from trade policies, exchange rate movements, or structural reform policies such as privatization. In sum, it is likely that the between effect is mostly driven by exogenous changes in the sector structure of the economy, while the within

Box 3.2

A Between-Within Decomposition for Employment Changes

To disentangle whether changes in employment of workers with different skills are driven mainly by changes in the sector composition of production and employment (the between effect) or by changes in the relative use of different types of skilled labor within each economic sector or industry (the within effect), it is possible to carry out a decomposition of changes in the share of each type of labor in total aggregate labor. Following Katz and Murphy (1992), define

$$\Delta\left(\frac{E_k}{E}\right) = \underbrace{\sum_j \alpha_{kjt}\Delta\theta_j}_{Between\ Effect} + \underbrace{\sum_j \theta_{jt'}\Delta\alpha_{kj}}_{Within\ Effect}$$

where E is the total amount of all types of labor used in the economy (in efficiency units), E_k is the total amount of labor of skill type k used in the economy (that is, $k =$ skilled or unskilled), j indexes the economic sectors, $\alpha_{kjt} = E_{kjt}/E_{jt}$ is input k's share of total employment in sector j at the base year t, and $\theta_{jt} = E_{jt}/E_t$ is the participation of sector j in total employment, also at time t. To implement these sector decompositions, 10 aggregate sectors or industries in each country are used: (a) primary activities (agriculture, forestry, fishing, mining, and quarrying); (b) low-technology manufacturing industries (food, beverage and tobacco, textile, and clothing); (c) other manufacturing industries; (d) construction; (e) retail and wholesale trade, repair, accommodation, and food services; (f) electricity, gas and water supply, transport, and communication; (g) financial sector, insurance sector, and professional services; (h) public administration and defense; (i) education and health; and (j) domestic services.

The first term of the decomposition, the "between effect," captures the impact of transformations in the sector structure of employment on the relative employment of a given factor (in this case, skilled labor). Suppose that, triggered by changes in international prices, sector m expands while sector n shrinks. If sector m is skill-intensive while sector n is the opposite, the change in the structure of the economy (in terms of sector employment) will favor skilled labor. The second term, the "within effect," captures changes in the use of different skill types of labor within each sector or industry.

It is important to recall that this methodology does not measure changes in demand for labor, but rather changes in equilibrium quantities (the result of both supply and demand changes). There might be exogenous sources of changes in

(continued next page)

Box 3.2 *(continued)*

both between and within factors, but also changes driven by changes in factor prices. Katz and Murphy (1992) and others argue that the "between effect" will likely reflect changes resulting from trade policies, exchange rate movements, or structural adjustment policies such as privatization. In contrast, the "within effect" may be due to many factors, including skill-biased technological change, adjustments of relative factor use due to changes in factor prices, changes in the relative labor supply, and institutional changes that cause changes in factor prices.

Source: Authors.

effect captures exogenous skill-biased technological change and also reflects adjustments in relative factor use, in response to changes in factor prices.

LAC has experienced important shifts in the sector composition of output over the past two decades. Since industries differ in their combination of skilled and unskilled labor, changes in the sector composition of output can lead to changes in the relative demand for different types of labor. Such changes can be generated by trade policy and market reforms that alter the relative price of goods or by changes in international prices. In the 1990s, most of the region experienced a major economic transformation linked to trade liberalization, privatization, and modernization of their economies. There was a surge in the service sectors at the expense of agriculture and manufacturing, except in Central America, where the *maquila* model gained ground and thus revitalized the manufacturing sector (figure 3.13).

In contrast, during the 2000s, many LAC countries (most notably the Andean subregion) saw an increase in mining and construction linked to the expansion of China and the surge in the demand for natural resources (figure 3.14). For other sectors, the pattern varies across the region. In the Southern Cone (Argentina, Paraguay, and Uruguay) there was a shift toward agriculture driven by high commodity prices. In most countries in LAC, except for Argentina and Uruguay, manufacturing continued its relative decline. Across the region, services declined in relative importance, except in Central America, where they continued an upward trend (especially in Costa Rica and Panama).

In terms of employment, there have also been changes in the 2000s in the sectors that drive most of employment creation (figure 3.15). With the exception of primary activities (mainly mining) in Peru and

Figure 3.13 Percentage Changes in Sector Shares of Gross Domestic Product, 1993–2001

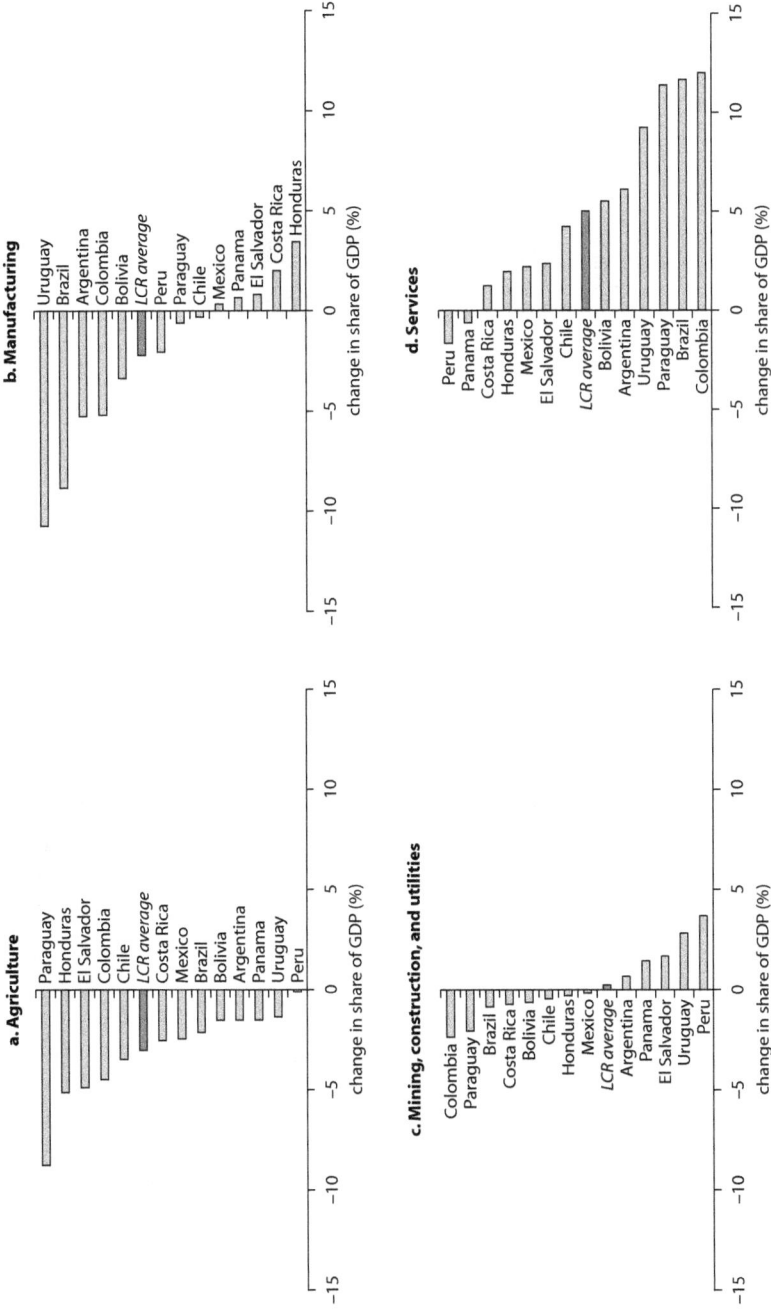

a. Agriculture

Paraguay
Honduras
El Salvador
Colombia
Chile
LCR average
Costa Rica
Mexico
Brazil
Bolivia
Argentina
Panama
Uruguay
Peru

change in share of GDP (%)

-15   -10   -5   0   5   10   15

b. Manufacturing

Uruguay
Brazil
Argentina
Colombia
Bolivia
LCR average
Peru
Paraguay
Chile
Mexico
Panama
El Salvador
Costa Rica
Honduras

change in share of GDP (%)

-15   -10   -5   0   5   10   15

c. Mining, construction, and utilities

Colombia
Paraguay
Brazil
Costa Rica
Bolivia
Chile
Honduras
Mexico
LCR average
Argentina
Panama
El Salvador
Uruguay
Peru

change in share of GDP (%)

-15   -10   -5   0   5   10   15

d. Services

Peru
Panama
Costa Rica
Honduras
Mexico
El Salvador
Chile
LCR average
Bolivia
Argentina
Uruguay
Paraguay
Brazil
Colombia

change in share of GDP (%)

-15   -10   -5   0   5   10   15

Source: Authors' calculations based on World Development Indicators 2011.
Note: GDP = gross domestic product.

Figure 3.14   Percentage Changes in Sector Shares of Gross Domestic Product, 2001–09

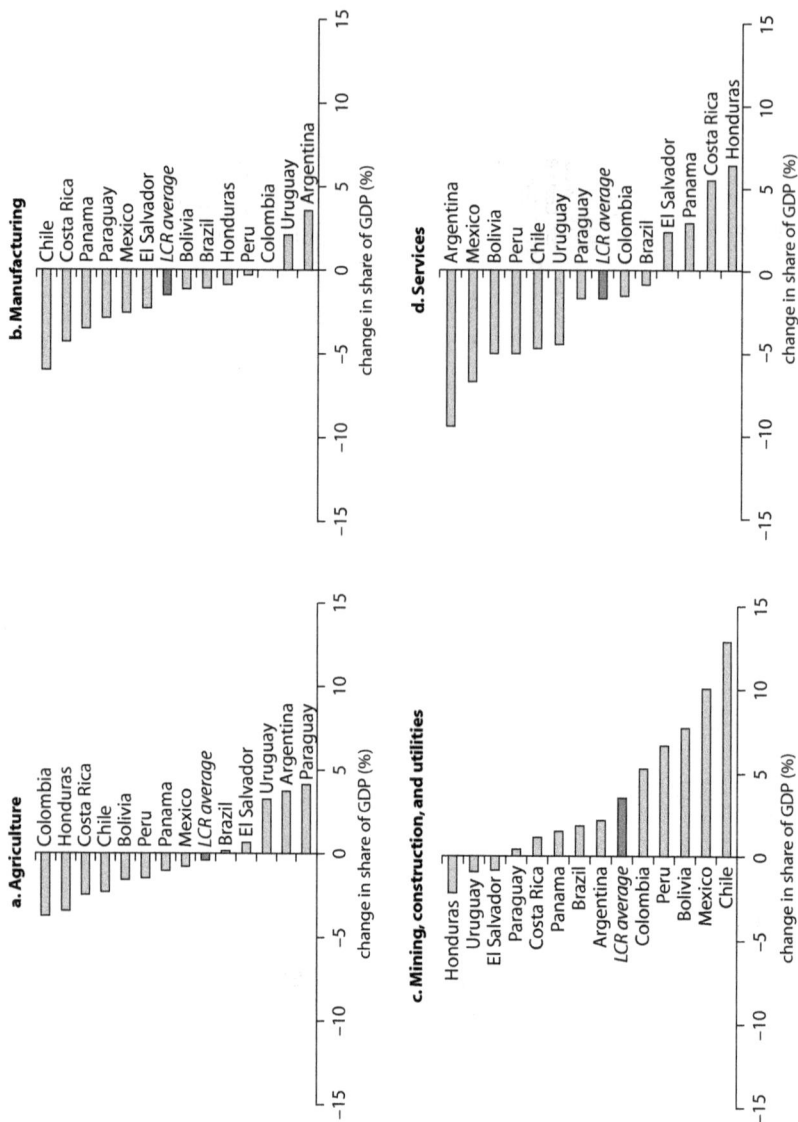

a. Agriculture

b. Manufacturing

c. Mining, construction, and utilities

d. Services

Source: Authors' calculations based on World Development Indicators 2011.
Note: GDP = gross domestic product.

Figure 3.15   Percentage Changes in Sector Shares of Employment, Selected LAC Countries, between 1996–99 and 2006–09

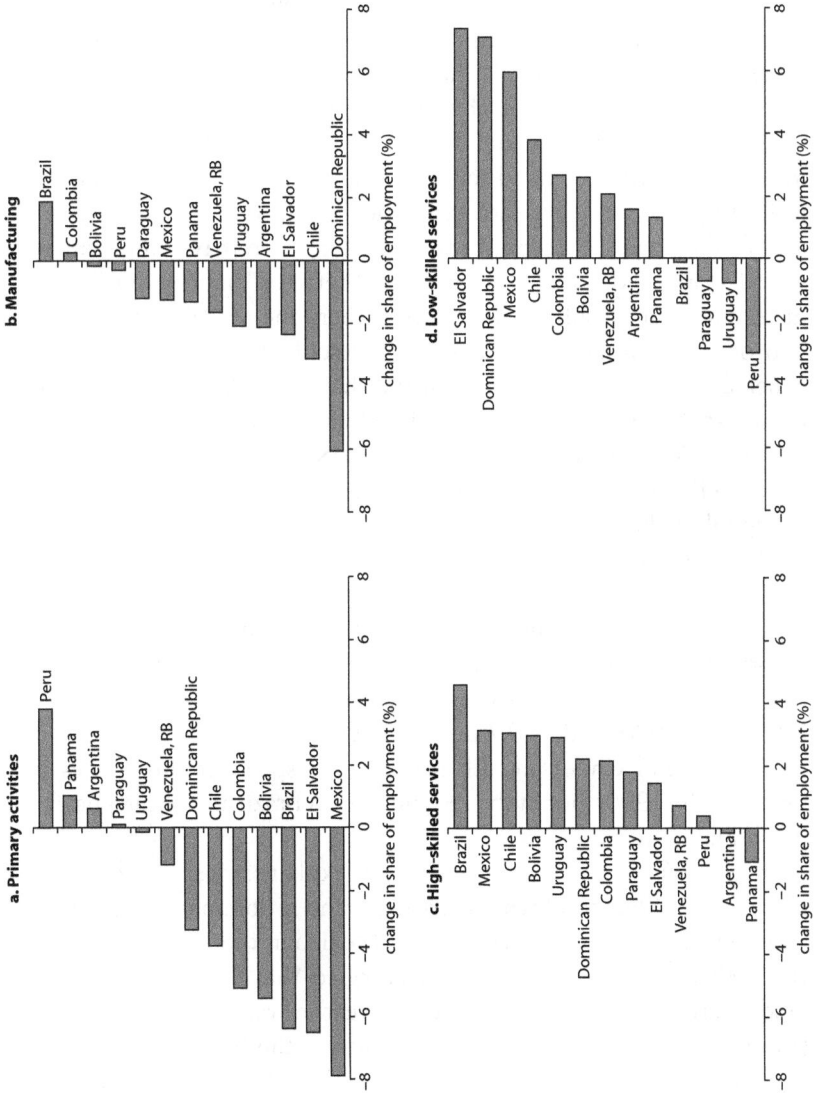

a. Primary activities

b. Manufacturing

c. High-skilled services

d. Low-skilled services

Source: Socioeconomic Database for Latin America and the Caribbean.

manufacturing in Brazil, most of the new jobs created in the countries in the region corresponded to services of both a high-skilled nature (finance, real state, education, health, and public sector) and a low-skilled nature (construction, retail, transport, and domestic services). There is no clear correlation between the evolution of educational wage premiums and the expansion of high-skilled or low-skilled service employment, with wage premiums declining in countries that largely expanded employment in both types of sector.

If the expanding service sectors were relatively intensive in high-skilled labor, while mining and construction were relatively intensive in low-skilled labor, this fact could help explain the decline in the relative demand for skilled labor. In this case, we would expect to find that the between-sector effect would be positive in the 1990s (reflecting an increase in relative demand for skilled labor) and negative in the 2000s (reflecting a decrease in relative demand for skilled labor). To explore this idea further, figure 3.16 presents changes in the relative employment of skilled workers, decomposed into both "between" and "within" employment effects, for a subset of countries where the available data span the two decades (using the methodology described in box 3.1). The first panel shows the annual change in the share of skilled labor in employment for the between-sector and within-sector components for the 1990s, while the second panel does the same for the 2000s. The "within effect" reflects factors such as skill-biased technological change, changes in capital or skill complementarities, or the creation or removal of labor market distortions favoring a particular skill group.

The share of tertiary-educated workers in total employment increased in all economies over time, consistent with the evidence presented in this report on the education upgrading in the region. On average, the proportion of tertiary educated workers increased by 0.6 percent per year in LAC in the 1990s and by 0.7 percent in the 2000s. In the Southern Cone (Argentina and Chile) and El Salvador, the speed of this process was higher in the 1990s, but in the rest, notably in Brazil and Nicaragua, it was much higher in the 2000s.

In general, the within-sector effect explains most of the relative increase in skilled employment creation, and it dominates the between-sector effect. The only exceptions are Mexico in the 1990s and Chile in the 2000s. For Mexico, the 1994 entry to the North American Free Trade Agreement was a trend-reversal year in wage premium evolution (as seen in figure 3.12). For most countries, the between-sector effect was more important in the 1990s than in the 2000s. But contrary to our

Figure 3.16   Change in Employment of Skilled Workers, and Between- and Within-Sector Composition, Selected LAC Countries, 1990s and 2000s

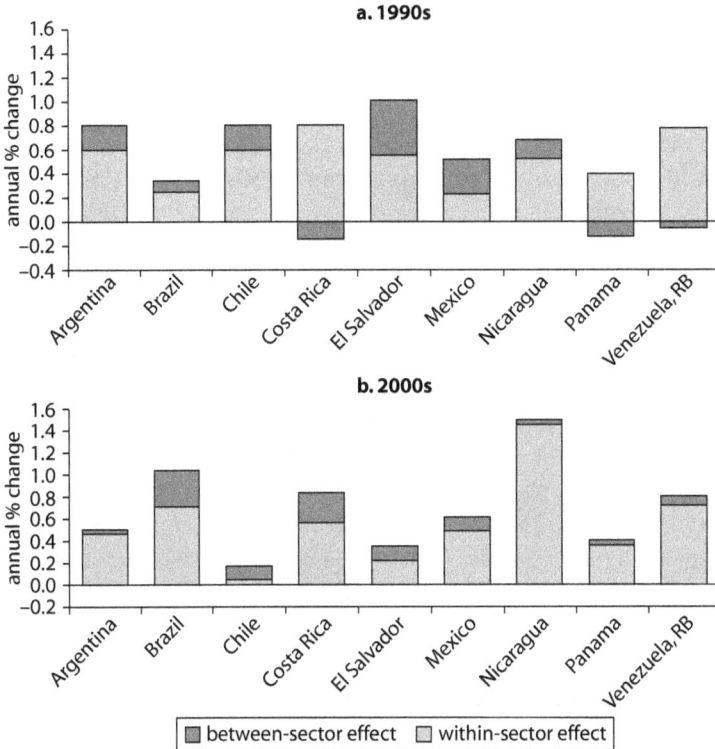

a. 1990s

b. 2000s

■ between-sector effect   □ within-sector effect

Source: Authors' calculations based on household surveys. Details on sample years, survey, and methodology are available in Acosta and others 2011.

expectations, the between-sector effect is positive in all countries in the 2000s (in the 1990s, the sign changes by country). For instance, Brazil, Chile, Costa Rica, and El Salvador experienced important skill-using between-sector employment effects, possibly associated with the expansion of high-technology sectors and attraction of foreign direct investment.

The implication of these findings is that the reduction in relative demand for skilled labor in the 2000s must then be mostly due to within-sector changes and not to between-sector labor reallocations. Changes within sectors could respond to technological change or to labor market distortions. As suggested by Goldin and Katz (2007), one possibility is that technology that was initially complementary to high-skilled workers, such as computers or other information and communication technologies, could have entered a period of diffusion where less-skilled workers could operate it. Another possibility is that labor market distortions might have weakened the link between productivity and pay. For example, the increases in real minimum wages experienced in Argentina, Brazil, Chile, and Uruguay could also generate wage compression within sectors.

We conclude from this analysis that the most important factor driving the reduction in skill premiums in the 2000s has been a slowing of demand growth for skilled labor, while the supply of skilled labor has continued growing at a steady pace. This is good news, since it means that the declining premiums could reflect the easing of a relative shortage, which was previously generating artificially high returns to tertiary education and constraining profitability and growth. The fact that within-sector or within-industry changes can explain most of the decline in premiums in the 2000s is consistent with a story about a shifting pattern of technical change (away from the skill-biased technical progress of the 1990s). However, this analysis cannot exclude the possibility that some part of the decline in premiums is related to other factors that affect workers in all industries the same way, such as quality issues in education and training programs, or institutional factors (such as minimum wages). We turn to these issues in the following sections.

Institutional Drivers: The Role of Minimum Wages[10]

The previous sections have presented evidence on how the balance of supply and demand for skilled labor and education quality issues have affected skill premiums in LAC over the past two decades. Skill premiums can also be affected by the laws and institutions governing labor markets. Legal minimum wages are an important institution in many Latin American countries, and in the past decade real minimum wages have risen sharply in almost all countries (figure 3.17).

Numerous recent studies have found that minimum wages compress the distribution of wages among employees in Latin America.[11] This compression happens because they have a bigger impact on the wages in the bottom part of the distribution than on those higher up. Since low-wage workers are likely to be less educated, increases in the minimum wage tend to increase the earnings of less educated employees relative to better-educated employees, leading to a fall in skill premiums.

Most studies of the impact of legal minimum wages in LAC present kernel density estimates of the distribution of the log of earnings, which

Figure 3.17   Evolution of Real Minimum Wages, Selected LAC Countries, 1995–2007

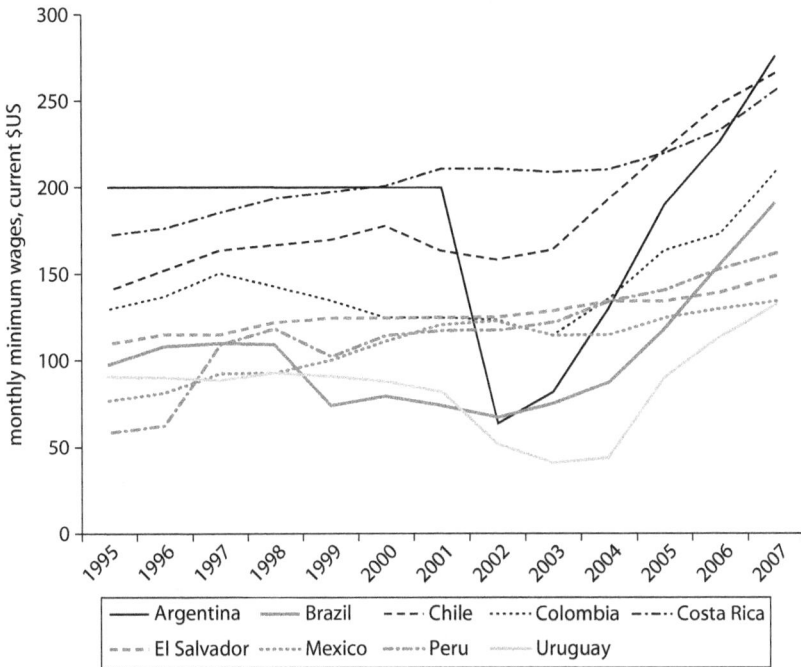

Source: ILO 2008.

show censoring of the distribution below the minimum wage. There is typically a spike in the distribution at the level of the minimum wage, suggesting that some workers who would earn below the minimum wage have their wages raised to the minimum wage. Maloney and Nunez (2004) present examples of kernel density estimates of the earnings distribution for formal and informal employees in six of the countries that we study: Argentina, Brazil, Chile, Colombia, Mexico, and Uruguay. They show that in all countries the minimum wage compresses the distribution of earnings, bringing the wages of low-wage workers (presumably less educated) closer to those of high-wage workers (presumably more educated).

Two studies explicitly measure whether the impact of minimum wages differs depending on the education level of the worker. Gindling and Terrell (2007) estimate the impact of higher minimum wages on the hourly wage of workers in different deciles of a distribution of "skills" in

Costa Rica. They find that minimum wages have a statistically significant impact on the wages of workers in the 2nd through 5th deciles. Workers in these deciles in the "skill" distribution have an average of six years of completed education or less, suggesting that minimum wages have an impact on the wages of workers with a primary education, but not with higher levels of education. Gindling and Terrell (2009) show that higher minimum wages significantly affect the wages of workers with primary and secondary education in Honduras, and that the positive impact on wages is largest for those with a primary complete education, while minimum wages have no statistically significant impact on the wages of workers with a university education.

Other recently published papers provide econometric evidence that changes in minimum wages have had an impact on inequality in the distribution of earnings in two Latin American countries. Bosch and Manacorda (2010) find that falling real minimum wages in Mexico were an important contributor to rising earnings inequality in the late 1980s and late 1990s. Several papers also present convincing evidence that increases in the real minimum wage were an important causal factor in the fall in earnings inequality in Brazil from the mid-1990s to the mid-2000s (Firpo and Cortez-Reis 2006; Barros and others 2010).

This brief literature review suggests that increases in the real value of the minimum wage should be correlated with falling education earnings premiums. Figure 3.18 presents evidence that trends in real minimum wages are indeed negatively correlated with trends in earnings premiums for workers with a secondary education in most LAC countries. The panels compare the evolution of the index of real minimum wages and changes in the earnings premiums for secondary and university graduates. Real minimum wages increased in the later part of the 1990s and throughout the 2000s in most of the LAC countries (except Costa Rica, El Salvador, and Mexico).

Countries where increasing minimum wages are correlated with falling earnings premiums for workers with a secondary degree include Brazil, Colombia, Nicaragua, and Peru. This fact is consistent with the hypothesis that increasing real minimum wages contributed to falling earnings premiums for workers with a secondary degree in these countries. In Mexico, falling real minimum wages from 1992 to 1996 are accompanied by stable earnings premiums for secondary graduates. Then, from 1996 to 2008, after real minimum wages stop falling, earnings premiums for secondary workers fall. This is consistent with the hypothesis that falling minimum wages were a cause of rising earnings premiums for secondary

Figure 3.18 Comparison of Real Minimum Wage Index with Secondary and University Earnings Premiums, Selected LAC Countries

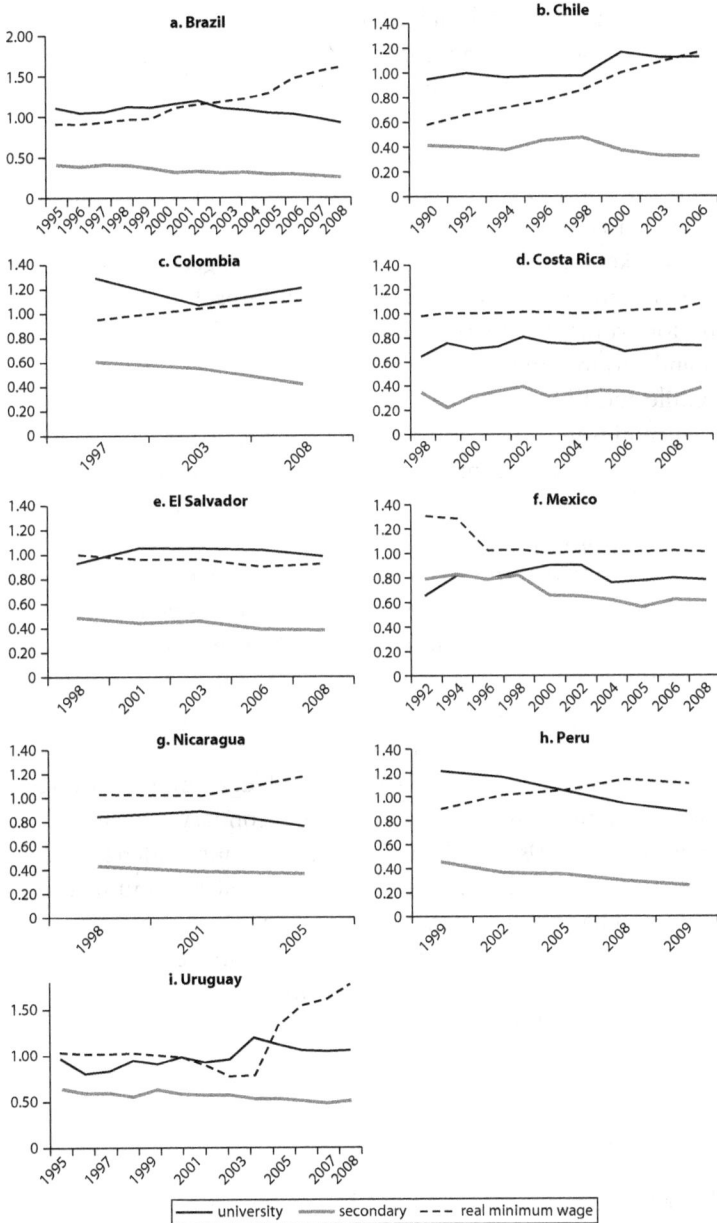

Sources: ILO, Regional Office for Latin America and the Caribbean, Panorama Laboral: América Latina y el Caribe (2000, 2006 and 2010), Gindling (2011).

Note: The y axis shows the relative increase in earnings for university-educated workers' earnings, compared with those of secondary-educated workers, and the relative increase for secondary-educated workers, compared with those with primary education. For example, a value of 0.4 indicates earnings that are 40 percent greater. The axis also shows the value of an index for the real minimum wage, with the year 2000 = 1.00.

education in the early and mid-1990s (and is consistent with the results presented in Bosch and Manacorda 2010), and that when real minimum wages stopped falling this change caused earnings premiums for secondary education to fall.

In Costa Rica, an agreement between the government and civil society groups in the late 1990s (*concertación nacional*) kept real minimum wages relatively constant from 1998 to 2008. Over this period, earnings premiums for workers with a secondary education changed very little. This fact suggests that minimum wages may have an impact on the earnings premiums for workers with secondary education (because real minimum wages and earnings premiums for secondary workers are stable).

In Chile and El Salvador, there is no evidence of a negative correlation between minimum wages and earnings premiums for workers with secondary education. In summary, in most countries the evidence is consistent with the hypothesis that increasing real minimum wages contributed to falling earnings premiums for workers with secondary education. In contrast, only in two of the 10 countries (Peru and Uruguay) are increasing real minimum wages correlated with falling earnings premiums for workers with a university education. Thus our evidence is generally not consistent with the hypothesis that rising real minimum wages are causing the changes in earnings premiums for workers with a university education.

We have presented evidence that is consistent with the hypothesis that in most LAC countries, increases in real legal minimum wages contributed to falling earnings premiums for secondary education in Latin America in the 1990s and 2000s. In contrast, our evidence is not consistent with the hypothesis that changes in legal minimum wages contributed to changes in earnings premiums for university-educated workers.[12] It is important to note that this evidence, based on simple correlations, is only suggestive; it is not sufficient to conclude that there is a causal relationship. More research is needed to establish a causal connection.

Notes

1. This section is based on a background paper for this regional study prepared by Tim Gindling and others (2011).

2. These household surveys (and the range of years for which data are available to us) are as follows: Brazil (Pesquisa Nacional por Amostra Domiciliar), 1995–2008; Chile National Socioeconomic Characterization Survey (Encuesta de Caracterización Socio-Económica Nacional, or CASEN), 1990–2006;

Colombia Quality of Living Standards Surveys (Encuesta de Calidad de Vida), 1998–2008; Costa Rica Household Surveys for Multiple Purposes (Encuesta de Hogares de Propositos Multiples), 1998–2008; Mexico National Survey of Income/Expenditure in Households (Encuesta Nacional de Ingreso-Gasto en Hogares), 1992–2008; Nicaragua Living Standards Measurement Surveys, 1998–2005; Peru National Household Surveys (Encuesta Nacional de Hogares), 1999–2009; El Salvador Household Surveys for Multiple Purposes (Enuesta de Hogares de Propositos Multiples), 1998–2008; and Uruguay Continuous National Household Surveys (Encuesta Continua de Hogares), 1995–2008.

3. Care should thus be taken when comparing our data with other sources, which often report the educational structure of the labor force for all workers aged 15 to 65.

4. For example, in Uruguay, the secondary cycle is divided into two stages, a mandatory three years (*ciclo básico*) and a nonmandatory three-year second cycle. During the past two years of the second cycle, students choose between three preundergraduate orientations: Biology, Law, or Math (ANEP-MEMFOD 2004).

5. This section is based on a background paper by Ana Maria Oviedo.

6. This section is based on Acosta and others (2011).

7. See the Socioeconomic Database for LAC and the Caribbean, jointly developed by Centro de Estudios Distributivos Laborales y Sociales at the Universidad Nacional de La Plata (Argentina) and the World Bank.

8. The definition of premiums used in this analysis is slightly different from that used in chapter 1. It differentiates between skilled labor (those with tertiary complete or incomplete) and the rest of the labor force.

9. The exceptions are Colombia and Costa Rica. However, even in these two countries the rate of growth in the relative demand for skilled labor was much slower in the 2000s than in the 1990s, so that while there was a continuous increase in demand for tertiary educated workers in the 2000s, the availability of skilled workers rose even faster.

10. This section is based on a background paper by Gindling (2011).

11. These include studies of most of the countries that we examine in this paper. Studies of Latin American countries include Argentina (Khamis 2008), Brazil (Lemos 2009; Neumark, Cunningham, and Siga 2006; Carneiro and Corseuil 2001; Fajnzylber 2001), Chile (Montenegro and Pages 2004), Colombia (Arango and Panchon 2004; Maloney and Nunez 2004), Costa Rica (Gindling and Terrell 2005, 2007), El Salvador (Gindling, Oviedo, and Trigueros 2010), Honduras (Gindling and Terrell 2009, 2010), Mexico (Bosch and Manacorda 2010; Cunningham and Siga 2006), Nicaragua (Alaniz, Gindling, and Terrell 2011), Peru (Jaramillo-Banante 2004), and Trinidad and Tobago (Strobl and

Walsh 2001). Almost all studies find evidence that minimum wages positively affect the earnings of employees in the formal sector. There is also some evidence from some countries that minimum wages affect the wages of workers in the informal sector. Some authors find a "lighthouse effect" where higher minimum wages appear to cause an increase in informal sector earnings: for example, in Argentina (Khamis 2008), Brazil (Carneiro and Corseuil 2001; Fajnzylber 2001; Lemos 2009), Colombia (Maloney and Nunez 2004), Costa Rica (Gindling and Terrell 2005), and Mexico (Cunningham and Siga 2006). Other studies find no impact of minimum wages on the wages of employees in the informal sector: for example, Honduras (Gindling and Terrell 2010) and Nicaragua (Alaniz, Gindling, and Terrell, forthcoming).

12. In Gindling (2011) we show that five of the countries that we studied have multiple minimum wages set by industry and/or occupation and/or education categories: Costa Rica, El Salvador, Mexico, Nicaragua, and Uruguay. In countries where there are multiple minimum wages, it is possible that the legal minimum wage for workers likely to have less education changes at a different rate than the minimum wage for workers likely to have more education. In this case, larger percentage increases in the minimum wage for less educated workers will result in falling education earnings premia. For example, Gindling and Terrell (2004) show that the introduction of a new minimum wage category for university-educated workers (which effectively increased the minimum wage for workers with university education) led to an increase in earnings inequality among private sector employees in Costa Rica in the early 1990s. However, Gindling (2011) presented evidence that changes in the structure of minimum wages in Costa Rica, El Salvador, and Nicaragua cannot explain the changes in education earnings premia in these three countries between 1998 and 2008 (data on changes in the structure of minimum wages in Mexico and Uruguay was not available).

References

Acosta, P., G. Cruces, S. Galiani, and L. Gasparini. 2011. "Educational Upgrading and Returns to Skills in Latin America: Evidence from a Supply-Demand Framework for the Decades of 1990 and 2000." Background Report, World Bank, Washington, DC.

Acosta, P., and L. Gasparini. 2007. "Capital Accumulation, Trade Liberalization, and Rising Wage Inequality: The Case of Argentina." *Economic Development and Cultural Change* 55 (4).

Alaniz, Enrique, Tim H. Gindling, and Katherine Terrell. forthcoming. "The Impact of Minimum Wages on Wages, Work and Poverty in Nicaragua." *Labour Economics*.

ANEP-MEMFOD. 2004. "Eficiencia interna de la Educación Secundaria Publica." Series Estudious Sociales sobre la Educación 10, ANEP, Uruguay.

Arango, Carlos, and Angelica Panchon. 2004. "Minimum Wages in Colombia: Holding the Middle with a Bite on the Poor." Unpublished paper, the Colombian Central Bank, Bogotá.

Attanasio, O., P. Goldberg, and N. Pavcnik. 2004. "Trade Reforms and Wage Inequality in Colombia." *Journal of Development Economics* 74: 331–66.

Barro, Robert, and Jong-Wha Lee. 2010. "A New Data Set of Educational Attainment in the World, 1950–2010." Working Paper 15902, National Bureau of Economic Research, Cambridge, MA.

Barros, Ricardo, Mirela de Carvalho, Samuel Franco, and Rosane Mendonca. 2010. "Markets, the State, and the Dynamics of Inequality in Brazil." In *Declining Inequality in Latin America: A Decade of Progress?* ed. L. López-Calva and N. Lustig, 134–74. Washington, DC: Brookings Institution Press.

Bosch, Mariano, and Marco Manacorda. 2010. "Minimum Wages and Earnings Inequality in Urban Mexico." *American Economic Journal: Applied Economics* 2 (4): 128–49.

Carneiro, Francisco Gairoa, and Carlos Enrique Leite Corseuil. 2001. "Minimum Wage Effects on Wages and Employment: Evidence from Time Series and Longitudinal Data." Working Paper 849, Institute for Applied Economic Research, Brasilia.

Cunningham, Wendy, and Lucas Siga. 2006. "Wage and Employment Effects of Minimum Wages on Vulnerable Groups in the Labor Market: Brazil and Mexico." World Bank, Washington, DC.

De Ferranti, David, and Guillermo Perry, Indermit Gill, J. Luis Guasch, William F. Maloney, Cardina Sánchez-Páramo, and Norbert Schady. 2003. *Closing the Gap in Education and Technology.* Washington, DC: World Bank, Latin American and Caribbean Studies.

Fajnzylber, P. 2001. "Minimum Wage Effects throughout the Wage Distribution: Evidence from Brazil's Formal and Informal Sectors." Unpublished paper, Department of Economics, Universidade Federal de Minas Gerais.

Firpo, Sergio, and Maurício Cortez-Reis. 2006. "Minimum Wage Effects on Labor Earnings Inequality: Some Evidence from Brazil." Mimeograph, Pontifica Universidade Católica, Rio.

Galiani, S., and P. Sanguinetti. 2003. "The Impact of Trade Liberalization on Wage Inequality: Evidence from Argentina." *Journal of Development Economics* 72: 497–513.

Gill, I., and C. Montenegro. 2002. "Responding to Earnings Differentials in Chile." In *Crafting Labor Policy: Techniques and Lessons from Latin America*, ed. I. Gill, D. Domeland, and C. Montenegro, 159–85. Washington, DC: World Bank.

Gindling, Tim H. 2011. "Can Minimum Wage Changes Help Explain Falling Education Wage Premia in Latin America?" Background paper, World Bank, Washington, DC.

Gindling, Tim H., Jose Andrés Oviedo, and Alvaro Trigueros. 2010. *Impacto de los salarios mínimos en el mercado de trabajo en El Salvador.* San Salvador: FUSADES. http://www.fusades.org/?cat=1543&lang=es&title=El+impacto+de+los+salarios+m%EDnimos.

Gindling, Tim H., and Katherine Terrell. 2004. "Minimum Wages, Inequality and Globalization." *Michigan Journal of International Law* 26 (1): 245–70.

———. 2005. "Legal Minimum Wages and the Wages of Formal and Informal Sector Workers in Costa Rica." *World Development* 33 (11): 1905–21.

———. 2007. "The Effects of Multiple Minimum Wages throughout the Labor Market: The Case of Costa Rica." *Labour Economics* 14: 485–511.

———. 2009. "Minimum Wages and Employment in Various Sectors in Honduras." *Labour Economics* 16 (3): 291–303.

———. 2010. "Minimum Wages, Globalization and Poverty in Honduras." *World Development* 38 (6): 908–18.

Goldin, C., and L. Katz. 2007. "The Race Between Education and Technology: The Evolution of U.S. Educational Wage Differentials, 1890 to 2005." Working Paper 12984, National Bureau of Economic Research, Cambridge, MA.

Harrison, A., and G. Hanson. 1999. "Who Gains from Trade Reform? Some Remaining Puzzles." *Journal of Development Economics* 59: 125–54.

ILO (International Labour Office). 2008. "Evolución de los salarios en América Latina, 1995–2007." Background paper for the *Global Wage Report 2008/2009*, Santiago de Chile.

Jaramillo-Banante, Miguel. 2004. "Minimum Wage Effects under Endogenous Compliance: Evidence from Peru." *Económica, La Plata* L (1–3): 85–123.

Katz, L., and K. Murphy. 1992. "Changes in Relative Wages, 1963–87: Supply and Demand Factors." *Quarterly Journal of Economics* 107: 35–78.

Khamis, Melanie. 2008. "Does the Minimum Wage Have a Higher Impact on the Informal than on the Formal Labor Market? Evidence from Quasi-Experiments." Discussion Paper 3911, Institute for the Study of Labor, Bonn.

Lemos, Sara. 2009. "Minimum Wage Effects in a Developing Country." *Labour Economics* 16: 224–37.

López-Calva, Luis F., and Nora Lustig. 2009. "The Recent Decline in Inequality in Latin America: Argentina, Brazil, Mexico and Peru." ECINEQ Working Paper 140, Society for the Study of Economic Inequality, Palma de Malorca, Spain.

———. 2010. *The New Dynamics of Income Inequality in Latin America.* Washington, DC: Brookings Institution and United Nations Development Programme.

Maloney, William, and Jaime Nunez. 2004. "Measuring the Impact of Minimum Wages: Evidence from Latin America." In *Law and Employment: Lessons from*

Latin America and the Caribbean, ed. J. Heckman and C. Pagés. Chicago: National Bureau of Economic Research, University of Chicago. http://ideas .repec.org/s/nbr/nberwo.html.

Manacorda, M., C. Sánchez-Páramo, and N. Schady. 2010. "Changes in Returns to Education in Latin America: The Role of Demand and Supply of Skills." *Industrial and Labor Relations Review* 63: 307–26.

Neumark, David, Wendy Cunningham, and Lucas Siga. 2006. "The Effects of the Minimum Wage in Brazil on the Distribution of Family Incomes: 1996–2001." *Journal of Development Economics* (Elsevier) 80 (1): 136–59.

Strobl, Eric, and Frank Walsh. 2001. "Minimum Wages and Compliance: The Case of Trinidad and Tobago." *Economic Development and Cultural Change* 51 (2): 427–50.

Tinbergen, J. 1975. *Income Distribution: Analysis and Policies*. North-Holland: Amsterdam.

CHAPTER 4

Education Quality and Student Achievement

This chapter focuses on the impact of expanded education coverage in Latin America and the Caribbean (LAC) on learning attainment, both in absolute terms and relative to other regions of the world. We analyze direct measures of cognitive human capital, documenting their evolution in the region based on the Program for International Student Assessment (PISA) test. We then analyze the determinants of these skills. The main message is that achievement has not, in general, been eroded by educational expansion. This is good news and is consistent with the conclusion of chapter 3, that it is demand-side factors rather than supply-side factors that have undermined earnings premiums in recent years. However, we also present worrying data on the size of the achievement gap between LAC and other regions, as well as the very slow pace of catch-up. These data suggest that the region needs a strong push to improve the quality of secondary education. The chapter closes with global benchmarking data on the relationship between spending per capita and PISA test scores, which suggest that many countries in LAC might find themselves in a "low quality equilibrium," where limited resources and poor efficiency in the use of the available funds reinforce one another to conspire against the step-change that is clearly needed in learning outcomes in secondary education.

Trends in Learning Achievement: Evidence from the PISA Tests[1]

International tests allow us to compare cognitive skills. The PISA test is administered to 15-year-olds who are enrolled in school, using a methodology that is comparable over time.[2] As well as collecting data on the students' academic attainment in reading comprehension, mathematics, and science, PISA also collects data on school characteristics and the household characteristics of the tested individuals. PISA assessments were carried out in 2000, 2003, 2006, and 2009. A growing number of LAC countries have participated, reflecting a shift in policy toward measuring education quality based on outcomes rather than inputs (table 4.1).

Based on PISA results, we discuss the following:

- Evolution of the average performance of LAC countries in PISA
- Evidence of changes in the efficiency of the LAC education systems in producing learning gains
- Analysis of within-grade efficiency
- Changing patterns of per grade school heterogeneity
- Distribution of education system gains by socioeconomic conditions of the students.

We analyze the factors driving improvements in student learning, showing evidence that increased efficiency in student promotion (age-grade correspondence) is an important source of gains. Because the potential for such gains is limited at the point where all students are in the right grade for their age, we also reflect on the underlying capacity of the education system to improve student learning within each grade

Table 4.1   Participation of LAC Countries in PISA

Countries	2000	2003	2006	2009
Argentina	X		X	X
Brazil	X	X	X	X
Chile	X		X	X
Colombia			X	X
Mexico	X	X	X	X
Peru	X			X
Uruguay		X	X	X
Panama				X
Trinidad and Tobago				X
Countries/ Economies In PISA	43	41	57	65

Source: Organisation for Economic Co-operation and Development (OECD).
Note: X means the country participated in PISA that year.

level. Finally, we analyze distributional aspects of recent gains in attainment, asking whether all types of student benefited equally.

Performance of LAC in PISA

LAC countries have improved over time, but they remain among the worst performers in PISA in both mathematics and reading.[3] Compared with the performance of Organisation for Economic Co-operation and Development (OECD) countries, the LAC performance lag in both tests is substantive. By 2009, the average performance of students from Argentina, Brazil, Chile, Mexico, and Peru was about 100 PISA points below the OECD in each test. This figure is the equivalent of a lag of two years of education (figure 4.1). In 2009, the 80th percentile in the LAC distribution performed at the level of the 37th percentile of the OECD

Figure 4.1   Comparison of LAC and OECD Countries in Performance Scores on PISA[a,b]

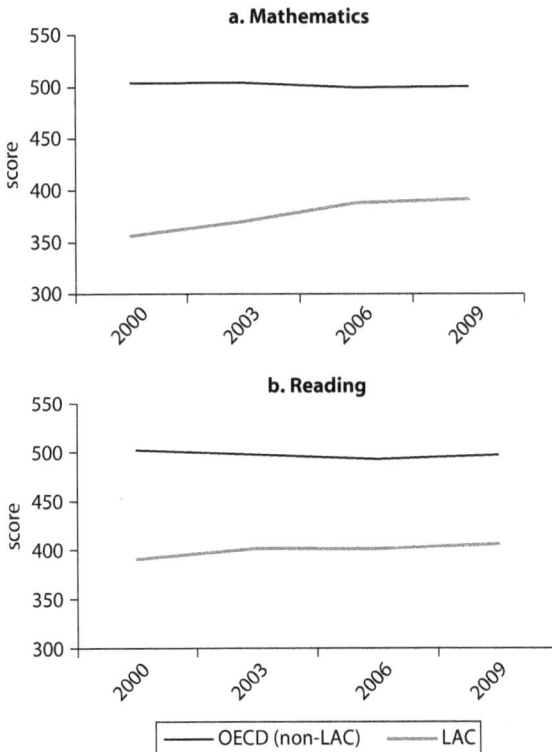

Source: Authors' elaboration based on OECD data.
a. LAC line represents the average performance of Argentina, Brazil, Chile, Mexico, and Peru in PISA.
b. The OECD's Program of International Student Assessment (PISA) is an international assessment of the reading, science, and mathematical literacy of 15-year-old students.

distribution in the mathematics test (up from the 24th percentile in year 2000) and in the 40th percentile of the OECD distribution in 2009 in the reading text (up from the 36th percentile in year 2000).

Overall, LAC PISA scores improved from 2000 to 2009, but the situation is heterogeneous across countries and tests. In mathematics, all countries show an overall improvement, apart from Argentina (which is stable). In reading, Chile, Colombia, and Peru improved their performance; Brazil and Mexico remained stable; and Argentina and Uruguay reported a decline (figure 4.2).

LAC's low performance relative to OECD countries can be explained, in part, by its lower level of economic development. However, LAC's performance is lower than would be expected for the level of gross domestic product (GDP) per capita, with almost all countries lying below the trend line (figure 4.3).

Figure 4.2   PISA Performance Scores, by LAC Country, 2000–09

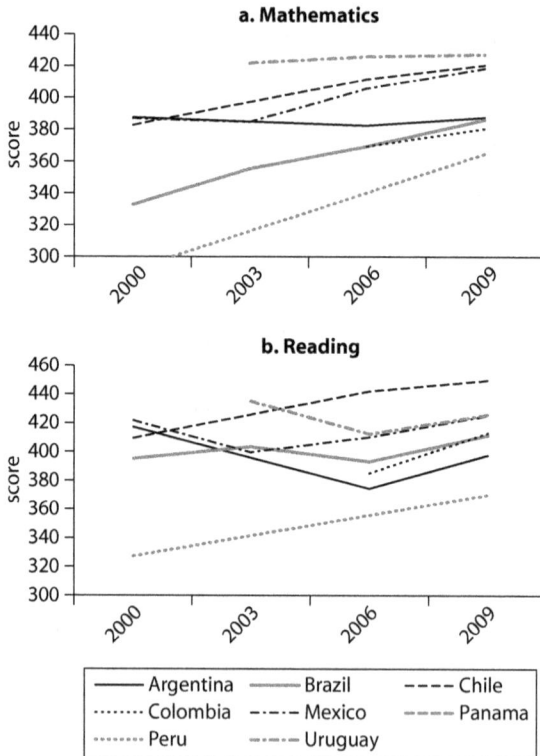

Source: Authors' elaboration based on OECD data.

Figure 4.3   PISA Performance Scores and Log GDP Per Capita, Selected LAC Countries, 2009

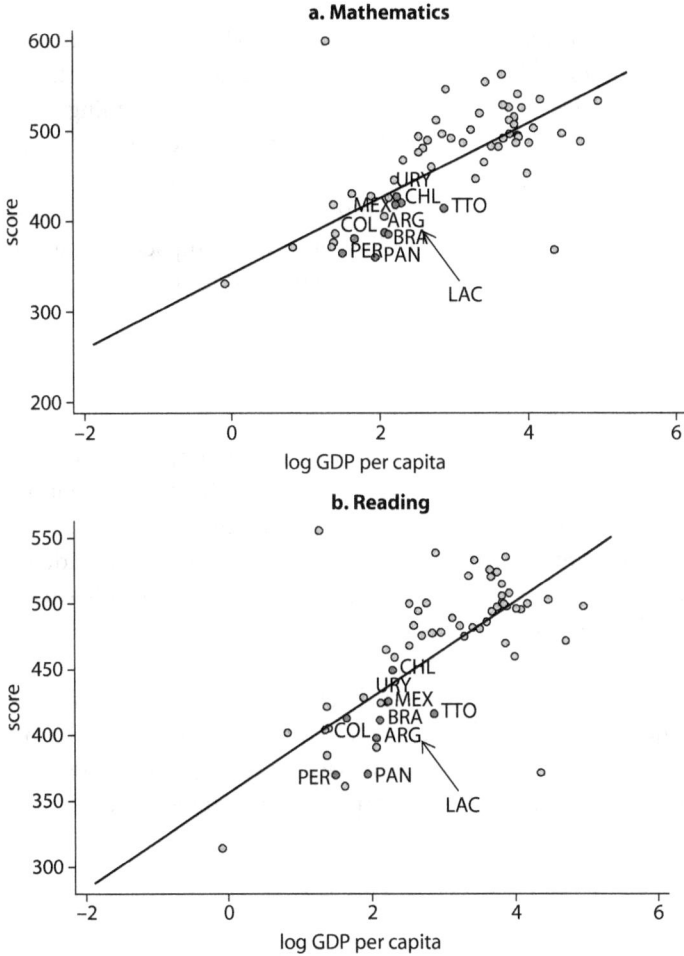

a. Mathematics

b. Reading

Source: Authors' elaboration based on data from OECD and EDSTAT.
Note: ARG = Argentina; BRA = Brazil; CHI = Chile; COL = Colombia; MEX = Mexico; PAN = Panama; PER = Peru; TTO = Trinidad and Tobago; URY = Uruguay.

Efficiency in Producing Learning Gains

Theory predicts that education results will depend on the interaction of family, school, and peer factors within an institutional setup that is designed to improve student results. It is often difficult to pinpoint the effects of specific inputs because data that combine all the necessary variables are lacking. PISA helps greatly in this regard by supplying data on results and inputs in the same dataset. In this section, we analyze the impact of the following inputs:

- *Student characteristics*, such as the grade in which the student is enrolled and the index of household socioeconomic conditions,[4] both of which are expected to have a positive impact on student learning
- *School characteristics*, such as the percentage of certified teachers, the principal's satisfaction with the supply of math teachers, the use of school-level assessments to monitor progress and teacher effectiveness (all of which are expected to have a positive impact on learning), and the student-teacher ratio (which is expected to have a negative impact above some threshold).

PISA tests are applied to a representative sample of 15-years-olds enrolled in school, at any grade level. In general, those students who have reached higher grades obtain better scores, so an improved grade-age correspondence can result in better PISA results. This result happens, not because students are learning more in a given grade, but because the education system is getting more efficient in promoting students. LAC countries differ considerably in the efficiency with which students are promoted between grades, as reflected in the average number of grades completed at age 15 (table 4.2).

Brazil and Peru have registered remarkable improvements between 2000 and 2009, while Argentina and Uruguay moved in the opposite direction. Table 4.3 shows the impact of changes in grade-age match at age 15 on the PISA score. Improved age-grade matches explain a

Table 4.2   Average Grade Attainment in PISA, Selected LAC Countries

	2000	2009
Argentina	9.6	9.4
Brazil	8.5	9.1
Chile	9.5	9.7
Mexico	9.4	9.5
Peru	9.3	9.8
	2003	2009
Uruguay	9.5	9.4
	2006	2009
Colombia	9.6	9.7

Source: Authors' elaboration based on data from OECD.

Table 4.3 Effect of Grade Attainment on PISA Mathematics Scores, Selected LAC Countries

Country	Base Year (BY) (STR_BY*SCORE_BY) A	Year 2009 (STR_09*SCORE_09) B	Adjustment (STR_09*SCORE_BY) C	% Explained by Grade Structure (C-A)/(B-A)
a. Base year 2000				
Argentina	387	388	366	–2,100
Brazil	334	386	355	41
Chile	383	421	398	40
Mexico	390	418	392	7
Peru	293	365	312	26
b. Base year 2003				
Uruguay	423	427	415	–200
c. Base year 2006				
Colombia	370	381	373	27

Source: Authors' elaboration based on OECD data.

Note: STR = estimated structure. The dependent variable is the Math PISA score. The independent variables are the index of socioeconomic conditions, share of certified teachers, student-teacher ratio, assessment of school progress, assessment of teacher effectiveness, dummy variable for lack of education materials, and dummy variable for the lack of math teachers. The base year is 2000 for Argentina, Brazil, Chile, Mexico, and Peru. The base year for Uruguay is 2003, and for Colombia it is 2006.

substantive portion (between 26 and 41 percent) of the learning gains in Brazil, Chile, Colombia, and Peru. But as commented above, there is a ceiling to potential learning gains from improved grade-age matches. Eventually, to sustain an increasing trend in PISA scores, it will be necessary to improve learning within a given grade.

Analyzing Within-Grade Efficiency

To isolate within-grade efficiency, we restricted our analysis to students in 10th grade in all countries (except Brazil, where 9th graders were analyzed).[5] The data for the base year (2000 for the cases of Argentina, Brazil, Chile, and Peru; 2003 for the case of Uruguay; and 2006 for the case of Colombia) were pooled. Using a regression framework, we look for evidence of changes in overall efficiency (changes in intercept) and changes in the efficiency of particular inputs (changes in slopes per input).[6]

Table 4.4 presents the estimation results of a fixed school effects model[7] for the mathematics scores. As already commented, there is suggestive evidence that Brazil, Colombia, Peru, and Uruguay present overall improvement in results after controlling for education inputs, while Argentina and Chile show an overall decline; the results for Mexico are not statistically significant. The index of socioeconomic conditions of schools and students has a positive effect on the PISA score. Lack of materials affects the learning process negatively in Argentina, Colombia, Peru, and Uruguay. The other regressors are not statistically significant for most countries. Interaction terms, in general, were not statistically significant, but their inclusion does result in a reduced impact of socioeconomic conditions in Brazil.

In an education production function framework, increased endowments of inputs with a positive expected impact should improve learning output, and vice versa. To assess the impact of changes in inputs on education outcomes, we present a counterfactual analysis that compares predicted outcomes for 2009 (modeled using coefficients for inputs from the base year) with the actual 2009 score. Table 4.5 compares predicted results with the observed 2009 PISA score for three different specifications. In some countries, the resources available in 2009 should have led to improvements in the PISA scores (Argentina), while in some cases, a decline in resources would have implied a fall in PISA scores (Brazil). However, Argentina's PISA score decreased despite the fact that the change in inputs predicted an improvement. In contrast, Brazil's score remained unchanged despite the negative predicted change. These results could reflect changes in systemwide variables and the impact of factors outside the education

Table 4.4   Random-Effect Model at the School Level, Mathematics PISA Results, Selected LAC Countries

	Argentina	Brazil	Chile	Colombia	Mexico	Peru	Uruguay
Year	**−20.81**	**20.36**	**−11.52**	**5.43**	−3.59	**27.57**	**21.00**
School-level Characteristics[a]							
Index of socioeconomic conditions	**63.66**	**50.90**	**61.31**	**42.16**	**42.36**	**64.23**	**39.39**
*Year	−3.36	**−15.43**	−4.39	6.48	1.12	−7.22	5.86
Share of certified teachers	−8.14	8.39	−19.93	11.49	20.76	**22.18**	**26.53**
*Year	26.46	**42.65**	4.05	−8.29	−33.03	−16.19	1.18
Student-teacher ratio	−0.65	**−0.75**	−0.08	**−0.58**	0.57	−0.18	0.32
*Year	0.26	0.49	0.12	0.19	−0.60	0.28	−0.13
Assessment of school progress	14.35	15.20	−4.14	n.a.	−2.53	9.13	−7.47
*Year	**−39.46**	−15.13	1.68	n.a.	−0.70	−7.55	**14.78**
Assessment of teacher effectiveness	11.88	−0.35	−4.04	−9.59	−14.29	4.30	0.30
*Year	−3.62	8.18	4.41	**12.35**	14.34	−8.53	3.31
Lack of materials	**−15.42**	−3.07	2.49	**−10.20**	−0.32	**−13.24**	**−7.75**
*Year	9.58	−1.44	−5.29	4.47	−2.19	4.12	6.35
Lack of math teachers	−1.90	−8.40	2.95	3.73	−0.78	−8.07	3.75
*Year	1.37	7.37	−2.05	−2.81	−1.78	2.01	**−6.19**
Individual-level characteristics							
Index of socioeconomic conditions	**12.08**	**5.98**	**4.69**	**9.02**	**5.92**	**14.43**	**6.91**
Year	0.91	−1.62	2.88	4.15	0.45	−3.85	**7.96**

Source: Authors' elaboration based on school effects and school-level characteristics as described by Mundlak 1978 and Green 2008.
Note: Dependent variable: mathematics score. Education production function: characters in bold significant at 5%.
* = Interaction variable between year and the variable mentioned.

system. For example, they might reflect efficiency gains in the education system because of better monitoring systems or other unobserved factors, such as more school days because of favorable weather conditions.

Changing Patterns of Within-Grade School Heterogeneity
Education production function analysis focuses on how differences in school performance are driven by differences in the socioeconomic conditions of students and by the educational inputs available to the schools.

Table 4.5   Comparison of Predicted and Actual PISA Results, Selected LAC Countries

	Base Year Score	Predicted 2009 Score[a]			Year 2009 Score
		Socio + School	Socio	School	
Argentina	426	445	446	432	418
Brazil	372	353	366	360	371
Chile	412	451	448	411	440
Colombia	395	403	401	397	404
Mexico	433	444	440	435	440
Peru	341	355	349	342	382
Uruguay	461	451	438	486	465

Source: Authors, based on Aedo and Luque 2011.
Note: The prediction is done using the regression coefficients of the base year.
a. Three different models were estimated. *Socio* includes the index of socioeconomic conditions. *School* includes the ratio of certified teachers, student teacher ratio, assessment of school progress, assessment of teacher effectiveness, dummy of lack of materials, and dummy of lack of math teachers. *Socio + School* includes all socioeconomic and school variables.

Table 4.6   School Heterogeneity: Within-Grade School-Level Effects, Mathematics, Selected LAC Countries

	Total		Controlled[a]	
	Base	Final	Base	Final
Argentina	60.20	54.37	30.58	35.64
Brazil	57.63	48.86	34.16	37.64
Chile	47.39	50.78	27.22	30.15
Colombia	47.90	41.73	35.01	26.59
Mexico	37.88	39.97	19.89	28.56
Peru	60.19	56.27	33.11	33.83
Uruguay	41.98	40.19	19.38	20.61

Source: Authors, based on Aedo and Luque 2011.
a. Results come from a random-effect model controlling for individual and school characteristics.

However, an important part of the variance is due to unobserved differences in the performance of teachers, principals, and other school-specific factors. This section asks if the divergence from the expected value has evolved in a homogeneous manner across schools and if the variance of schools' within-grade divergence from the potential level has been reduced.[8] We find that the evolution of variance has been mixed, increasing in some countries and decreasing in others (table 4.6). However, the heterogeneity not explained by school and individual characteristics has increased everywhere except in Colombia.

Based on the regression model estimated in the previous section, we plotted a school effect, defined as the difference between within-grade school achievement and the predicted value, for the base year (2000 for Argentina, Brazil, Chile, Mexico, and Peru; 2003 for Uruguay; and 2006 for Colombia). We compared the results in 2009 with the predicted value from the base year. Figure 4.4 presents the results for mathematics (figure 4.7 presents the results for reading). A shift in the curve toward the right indicates a positive deviation from the initially predicted value, and a shift toward the left indicates a negative deviation. In mathematics, there is an overall improvement in the distribution (that is, an unambiguous right-ward shift of the curve) for Brazil, Colombia, Mexico, Peru, and Uruguay, while Argentina and Chile present a clear deterioration. In reading, the

Figure 4.4   Analysis of Counterfactual Within-Grade School Effects, Mathematics, Selected LAC Countries

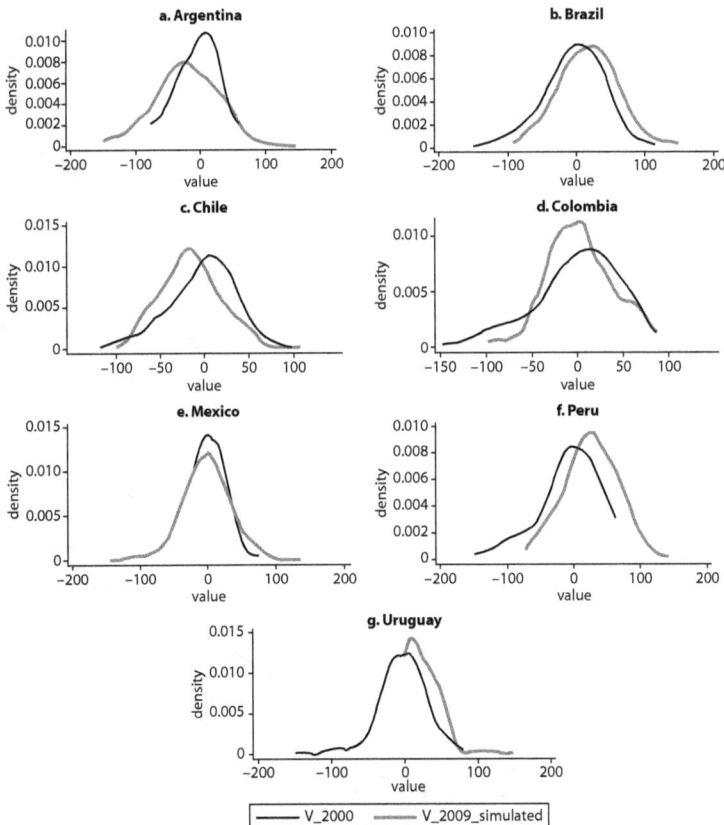

Source: Authors, based on Aedo and Luque 2011.
Note: The y-axis represents the density of PISA math scores based on observed data.

situation is reversed: only Colombia and Peru show an improvement in the distribution of within-grade school effects.

Education System Gains and Socioeconomic Conditions

The evidence suggests that all countries except Argentina increased their student achievement across the full range of the socioeconomic index (figure 4.5). Brazil, Chile, Colombia, and Mexico decreased the

Figure 4.5   Analysis of System Efficiency: Grade Attainment by Socioeconomic Conditions, 15-Year-Olds, Selected LAC Countries

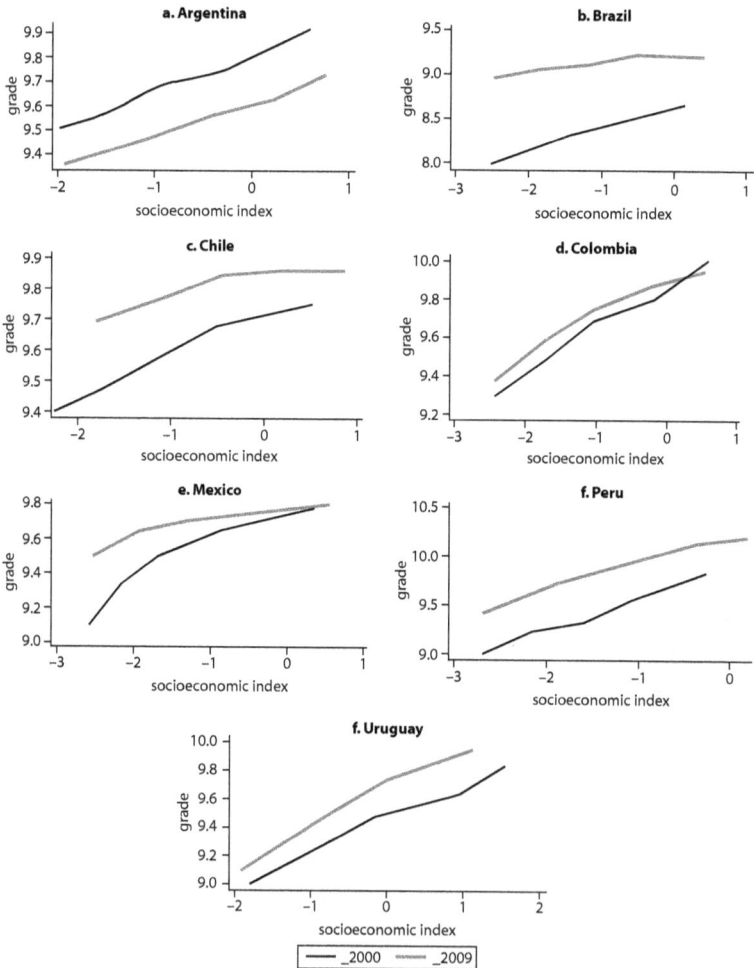

Source: Authors, based on Aedo and Luque 2011.

attainment gap (years of schooling) between the richest and the poorest socioeconomic groups. But in Argentina, Peru, and Uruguay the gap has been maintained.

For within-grade school effects in mathematics, the results are mixed (figure 4.6). Argentina, Chile, and Mexico decreased their expected performance between 2000 and 2009. In contrast, Brazil, Peru, and Uruguay increased their expected performance across socioeconomic

Figure 4.6   Analysis of Within-Grade School Effects: PISA Performance in Mathematics by Socioeconomic Conditions, Selected LAC Countries

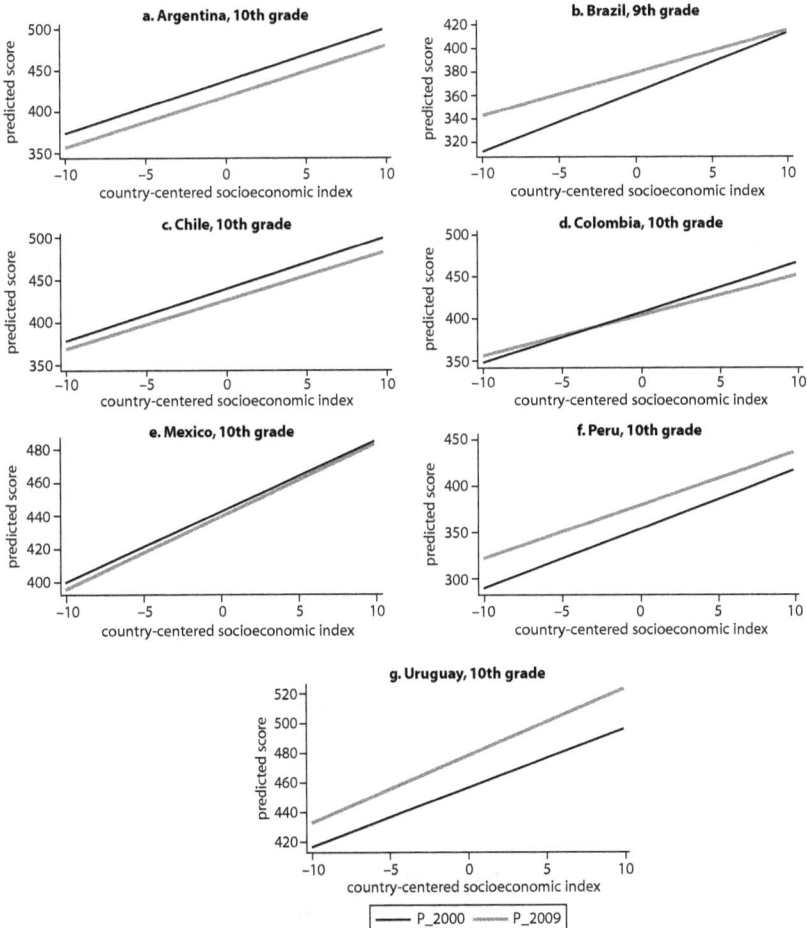

Source: Authors, based on Aedo and Luque 2011.

Figure 4.7   Analysis of Counterfactual Within-Grade School Effects, Reading, Selected LAC Countries

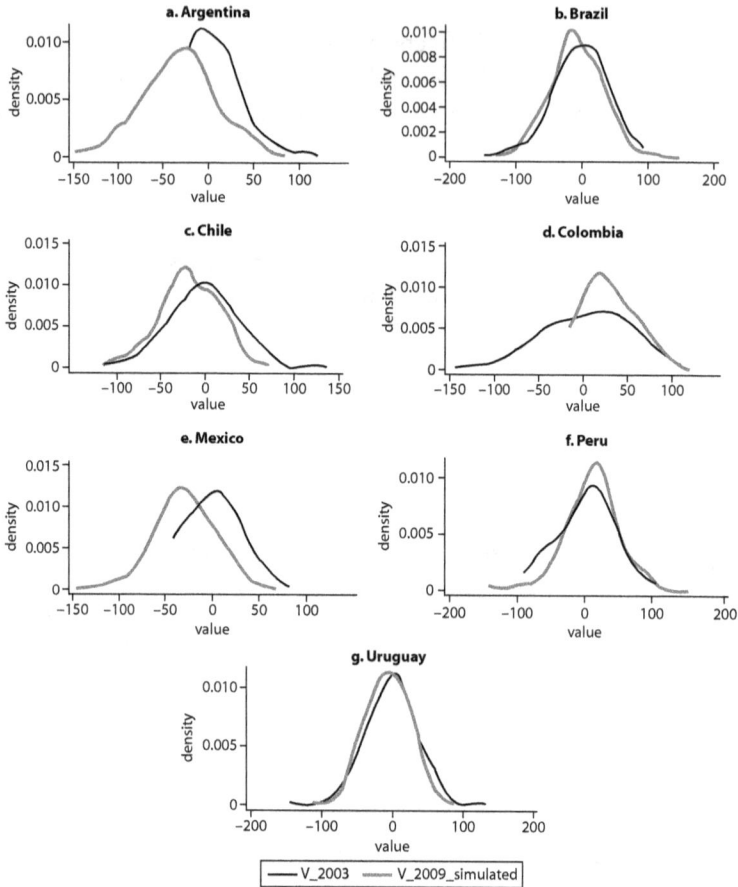

Source: Authors, based on Aedo and Luque 2011.
Note: The y-axis represents the density of PISA math scores based on observed data.

groups. Brazil, Chile, Colombia, and Peru reduced the performance gap between the richest and the poorest, while Uruguay was the only country that worsened the gap. In Argentina and Mexico, there was no change. In reading, only Colombia, Peru, and Uruguay improved their performance across socioeconomic groups, while the other countries worsened their predicted performance (figure 4.8). Brazil, Chile, and Peru reduced the performance gap between the richest and the poorest, while in Argentina, Colombia, and Uruguay the gap worsened. Mexico remained unchanged.

Figure 4.8   Analysis of Within-Grade School Effects: PISA Performance in Reading by Socioeconomic Conditions, Selected LAC Countries

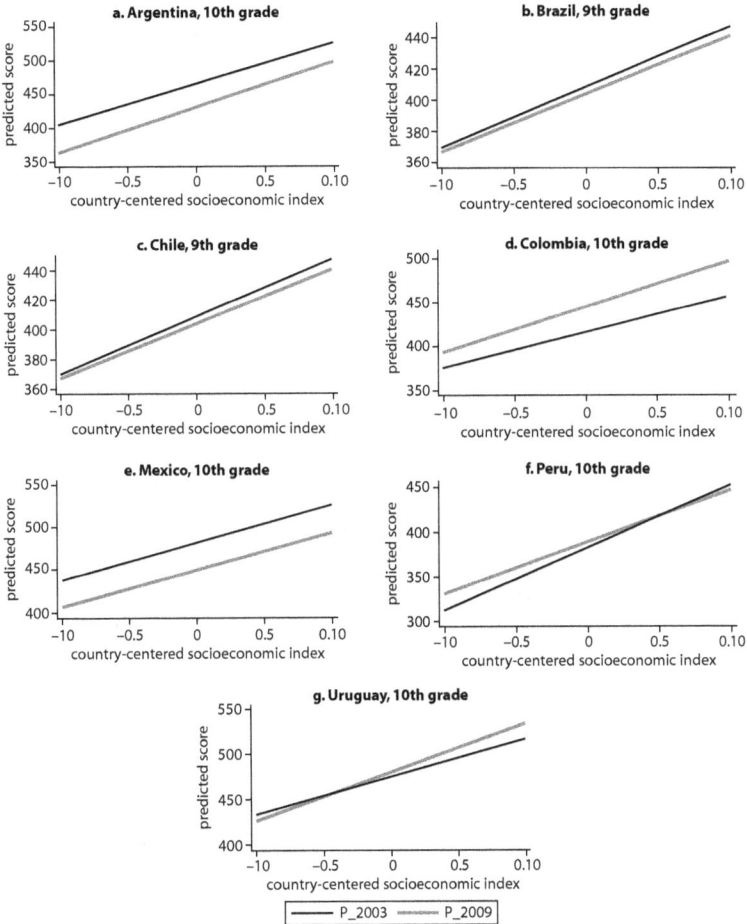

Source: Authors, based on Aedo and Luque 2011.

Benchmarking LAC's Performance on PISA

As noted in figure 4.3, LAC's performance on PISA looks weak in relation to per capita GDP. Other countries with similar levels of income did much better. That might be the result of spending more, the result of spending better, or some combination of the two. Demographics might also be an important part of the story: aging countries (with smaller population shares of school age) might have an advantage. In this section, we present additional benchmarking results, focusing on the relationship of spending per pupil to PISA scores, which provides a better sense of whether the problem is mainly related to ineffective spending or to the level of spending. Figure 4.9 plots PISA math scores against total education spending per pupil (standardized in terms of per capita GDP). The LAC countries are clustered well to the left, indicating that they have much lower levels of total education spending per pupil, relative to GDP, than most OECD countries. In this view, it appears that resource assignment might be an important aspect of the problem. In general, LAC's performance on PISA is well below the OECD mean, but it is scattered above and below the regression line. However, there are also important differences in outcomes within the LAC group, indicating that effectiveness in the use of resources is an important dimension of variance within the region, with Argentina, Brazil, and Colombia looking weak and Chile and Uruguay looking relatively good.

The comparability across countries of the data in figure 4.9 might be distorted by relatively high spending on university education in most OECD countries compared with LAC countries. University spending arguably has limited relevance to the determination of secondary outcomes.[9] Private spending is also included; private schools' performance and funding might both be very different from those of the public sector, and patterns might vary across countries and regions. Figure 4.10 plots PISA math scores against *total spending per pupil in secondary education*

Figure 4.9   Correlation of PISA Mathematics Scores with Total Education Spending Per Pupil, 2006

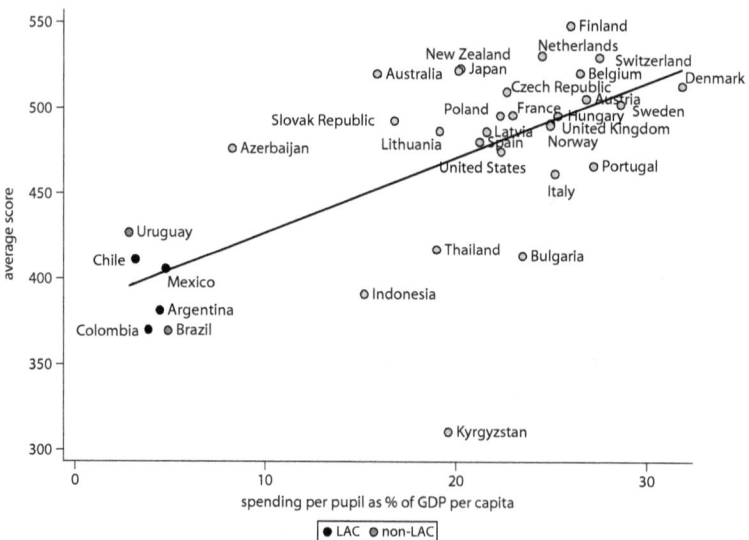

Source: UNESCO.

Figure 4.10   Correlation of PISA Mathematics Scores with Total Spending Per Pupil in Secondary and Nonuniversity Tertiary Education, 2006

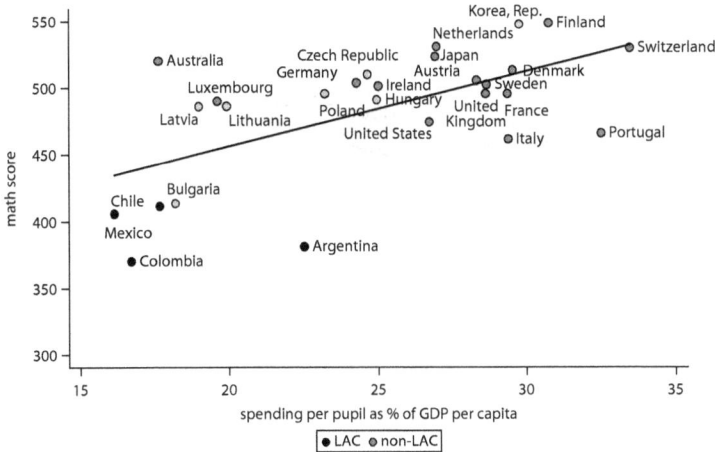

Source: United National Educational, Scientific and Cultural Organization (UNESCO) and World Bank.
Note:

and nonuniversity tertiary education. All the LAC countries, apart from Argentina, report lower spending per pupil than the OECD mean. However, some OECD countries (such as Australia and Luxembourg) whose levels of per student spending are similar to those of LAC register much better PISA scores. This fact suggests that the low achievement of LAC's students is explained by a combination of limited resources and inefficient spending. Figure 4.11 plots PISA math scores against *public spending per pupil in secondary education.* All the LAC countries, apart from Argentina, report much lower public spending per pupil in secondary education than the OECD mean. This finding might reflect, in part, the more important role played by private secondary education in LAC. But all LAC countries are also situated below the regression line, some of them (for example, Argentina and Colombia) are well below it. We can conclude that secondary education in LAC is less well resourced with public funds than OECD comparators. We can also conclude that the system as a whole is also less well funded and that it is performing badly on converting the public and private resources it has available into educational achievement on the metric of PISA scores. This situation looks like a classic case of low-quality equilibrium, where poor performance with the existing resources might make it hard to justify increased funding. The fact that the middle class often has access to better-quality private options might help to sustain the low-quality equilibrium by reducing pressure for change in public schools.

Figure 4.11   Correlation of PISA Mathematics Scores with Public Spending Per Pupil in Secondary Education, 2006

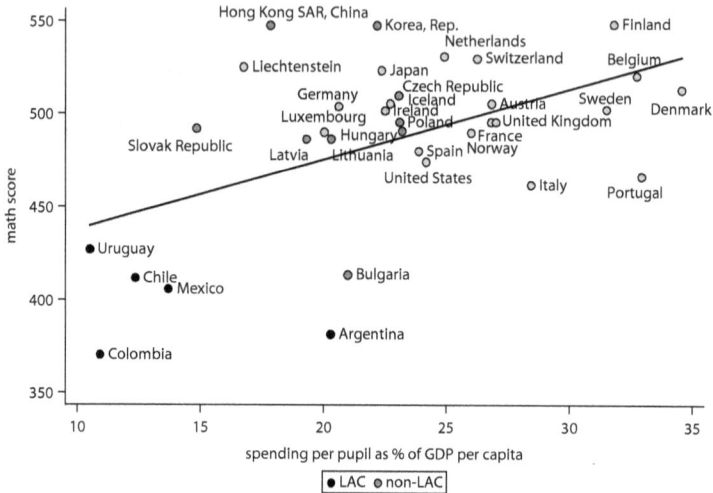

Source: UNESCO and World Bank.

Inferring the Trends in Tertiary Quality from Earnings Variance

Earlier we presented evidence on the academic attainment of 15-year-olds in secondary school based on the PISA test, concluding that quality has not deteriorated as the system has expanded but still remains poor compared to that in the OECD. Unfortunately, there is no analogous dataset that allows us directly to measure the learning achievement of tertiary graduates. In this section, we present indirect evidence on trends in tertiary quality.

If the expansion of tertiary education were eroding the average quality of graduates, we would expect to observe increased variance in earnings for tertiary graduates. This result might be due, for example, to increased variance in the quality of students (as educational expansion pulled in more students from the low end of the ability distribution) or to increased variance in teaching quality (the expansion of lower-quality universities or the hiring of lower-quality faculty). To explore this possibility, we examined trends in variance in earnings within education categories and their correlation with earnings premiums. Specifically, we constructed figures that compare changes in the coefficient of variation in earnings for university (and secondary) graduates to changes in their respective earnings premiums (figures 4.12 and 4.13, respectively). The figures do not

Figure 4.12   Comparison of Variation in Real Monthly Earnings to Earnings Premiums for Full-Time Workers with University Complete Education, Selected LAC Countries

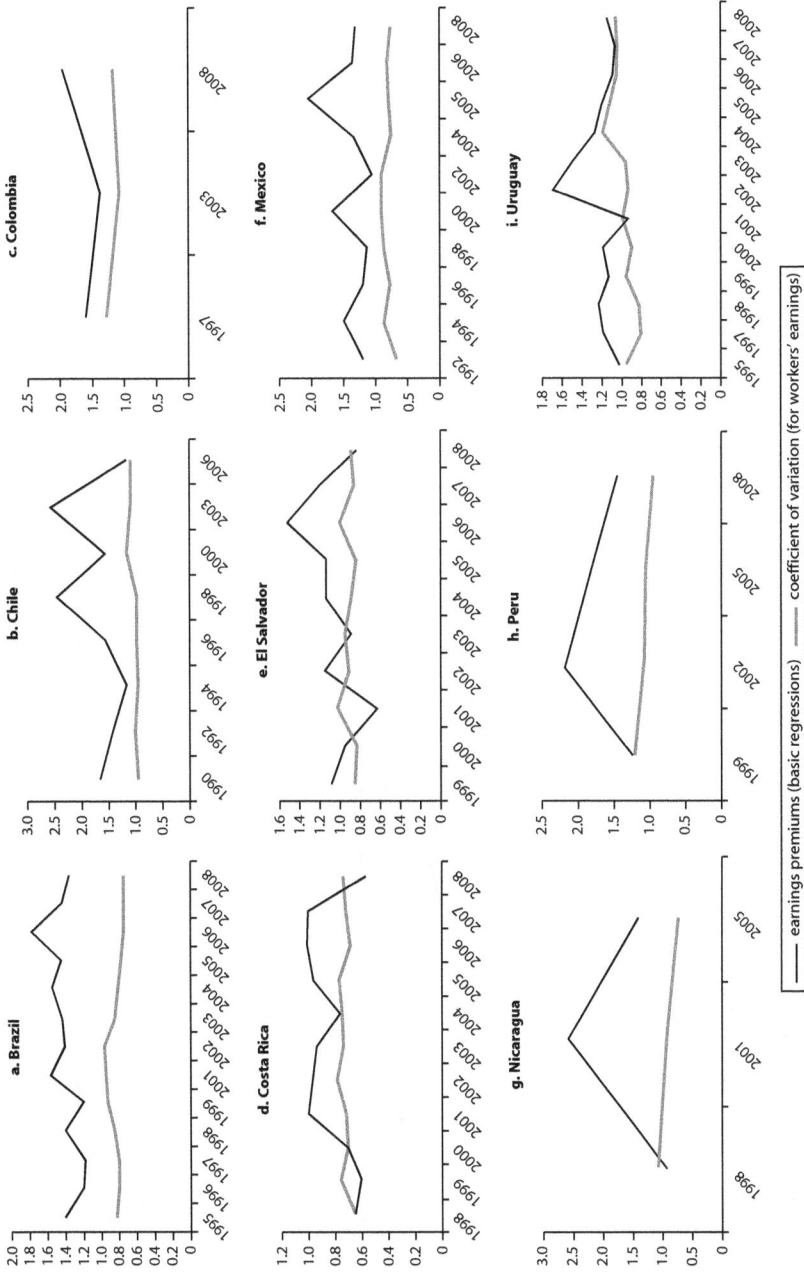

Source: Authors, based on Gindling and others 2011.

Figure 4.13 Comparison of Variation in Real Monthly Earnings to Earnings Premiums for Full-Time Workers with Secondary Complete Education, Selected LAC Countries

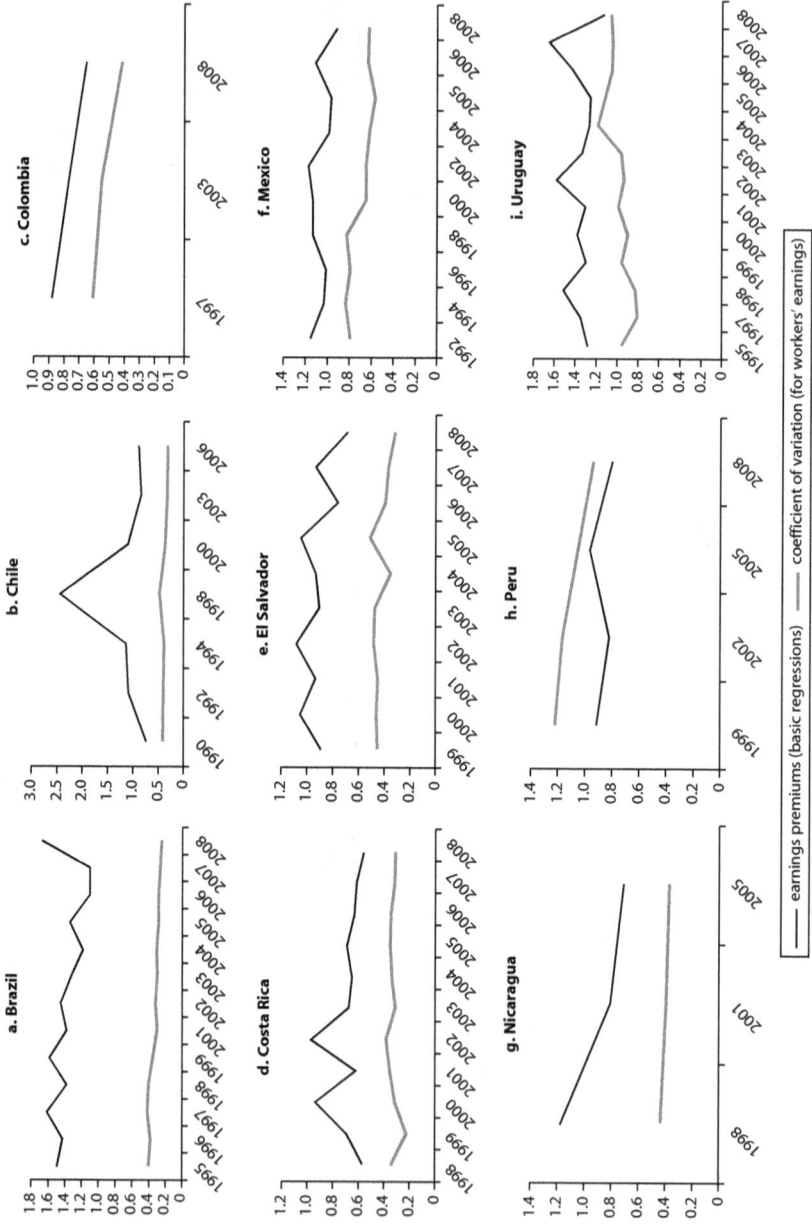

Source: Authors, based on Gindling and others 2011.

suggest that falling returns to university or secondary education are correlated with increasing variation in earnings; in fact, in some countries the opposite seems to hold. For example, in Brazil the variation in earnings for university graduates increases from 1995 to 2002 as earnings premiums for university graduates rise, and then falls from 2002 to 2008 as earnings premiums for university graduates fall. The same positive correlation between variation in earnings and earnings premiums can be seen in Colombia and Uruguay. In other countries, the variance in earnings tends to fall in a secular fashion, while earnings premiums sometimes increase and sometimes decrease.

Notes

1. This section is based on a background paper by Cristian Aedo and Javier Luque 2011.

2. LAC also has a regional comparative and explanatory assessment of the quality of student learning. The Latin American Laboratory for Assessment of the Quality of Education (LLECE) (1998) and the Second Regional Comparative and Explanatory Study (SERCE) (2008) have included for each country in the region samples of students in third and sixth grades. The Third Regional Comparative and Explanatory Study (TERCE) is currently being implemented, and its results will be available in 2013.

3. PISA also includes a science assessment. Those results are not reported in this paper because they do not change the overall conclusions of the analysis.

4. The index of socioeconomic conditions in the different versions of PISA are not strictly comparable. The team constructed a new index based on the education level of the student's father and mother and the number of books at home. The new index has the same mean and distribution as the PISA index for the base year.

5. These grades correspond to the highest enrollment per country in the PISA database. The focus on the most attended grade isolates the effect of socioeconomic conditions on grade attainment.

6. The analysis uses school effects and school-level characteristics as described by Mundlak (1978) and Green (2008). The following equation was estimated:

$$Y_{ijt} = \alpha_0 + \alpha_1 \, Year_t + \alpha_2 \, SES_{jt} + \alpha_3 \, SES_{jt} * Year_t + \alpha_4 \, (SES_{ijt} - SES_{jt})$$
$$+ \alpha_5 \, (SES_{ijt} - SES_{jt}) * Year_t$$
$$+ \dots\dots\dots\dots\dots\dots\dots +$$
$$+ \alpha_k \, Math_{jt} + \alpha_{k+1} \, Math_{jt} * Year_t + \mu_{jt} + \varepsilon_{ijt}$$

with

$E[\mu_{jt}] = 0$, all j and t; $E[\mu_{jt}\mu_{ks}] = 0$ if $j \neq k$ or $t \neq s$; and $E[\mu^2_{jt}] = \sigma^2$

$E[\varepsilon_{ijt}] = 0$, all i, j, and t; $E[\varepsilon_{ijt} \varepsilon_{rks}] = 0$ all $i \neq r$ or $j \neq k$ or $t \neq s$; and $E[\varepsilon^2_{ijt}] = v^2$

$E[\varepsilon_{ijt} \mu_{rk}] = 0$, all i, j, t, r, and k

SES_{jt} measures the index of socioeconomic status of the school j in year t, SES_{jit} measures the index of socioeconomic status of student i in school j in year t; $Math_{jt}$ represents the lack of math teachers as reported by the index of principal's satisfaction; μ_{jt} represents a fixed effect and ε_{ijt} represents a white noise. This equation also includes the following regressors: the percentage of certified teachers of school j in year t, the student-teacher ratio of school j in year t, whether the school uses assessments to monitor school progress in school j in year t, whether the school uses assessments to monitor teacher effectiveness in school j in year t, and the index of principal's satisfaction with the supply of classroom materials of school j in year t.

7. The model is estimated through random effects; that is, the school effects are realizations from a common distribution that is used to reduce estimation biases.

8. The first change implies a shift of the curve, while the second implies a change in the shape of the curve.

9. However, university spending it is not totally irrelevant to secondary school outcomes. It can influence them through the effect on children's achievement of having a more educated parent and through the effect on the availability and quality of secondary teachers (who are normally, but not always, trained at the tertiary level).

References

Aedo, Cristian, and Javier Luque. 2011. "Cognitive Trends in LAC: Recent Trends and Major Determinants. Evidence from International Tests." Report to the World Bank for Background Paper FY10, World Bank, Washington, DC.

Gindling, Tim H., with Camilo Bohórquez, Sergio Rodríguez, and Romero Barreto Rocha. 2011. "Trends in Education Quality and Labor Market Returns in Latin America: Evidence from Household Surveys." Report to the World Bank for Background Paper FY10, World Bank, Washington, DC.

Mundlak, Yair. 1978. "On the Pooling of Time Series and Cross Section Data." *Econometrica* 46 (10): 69–85.

OECD (Organisation for Economic Co-operation and Development). Programme for International Student Assessment. Available at http://www.pisa.oecd.org.

CHAPTER 5

Is Labor Demand in LAC Accommodating to Inferior Skills?

This chapter focuses on deepening our understanding of the underlying causes of the trends in skill premiums that were described in chapter 2. This understanding is critical to identifying appropriate policy responses to declining skill premiums. In the absence of evidence that education expansion is eroding quality (chapter 4), it seems probable that the decline in earnings premiums can be traced back to demand factors, as was suggested in chapter 3. But the pattern of labor demand is not necessarily exogenous: the market might learn to accommodate the type of skills offered. If so, the slowing of demand for more educated workers might be a response to the quality of skills. We present two blocks of evidence that give reason for concern that this response might be happening in Latin America and the Caribbean (LAC).

The first section shows that in the five LAC countries for which we have data (Brazil, Costa Rica, Mexico, Nicaragua, and El Salvador), the occupational pattern of employment has developed differently from that observed in the United States in the past two decades. There has been a greater expansion in LAC of work with relatively low skill requirements. The section applies a methodology developed by Autor, Levy, and Murnane (2003) that uses information about the specific skill requirements of different occupations in the United States and the occupational balance of total employment in LAC countries to impute the trends in overall demand for different types of skill. Autor, Levy, and Murnane's analysis for the United States showed an increase in the demand for "new economy" skills, that is, higher-level analytical and organizational skills. In contrast, our analysis for LAC shows that the main expansion is in jobs that (in the United States) demand traditional cognitive skills, such as those associated with tasks in manufacturing, while the use of higher-level skills has apparently flat lined. The question remains whether this outcome reflects the intrinsic demand characteristics of the region's economies or it is simply the result of the supply constraints in the labor force (with investment decisions adapting to the available skill endowment).

The second section presents evidence that LAC companies inserted into the global economy (as measured by factors such as technology adoption and export activity) are more likely to face problems recruiting the skilled labor they need. Enterprise survey data are analyzed to show that this class of firms takes significantly longer to fill available posts. This finding further supports the hypothesis that the available skill sets might be constraining the region's development in some areas of economic growth potential. The fact that other regions, such as East Asia, continue to increase the relative rewards of more educated workers, while they are declining in LAC, might suggest that these formal qualifications entail different skill sets in the two regions. It also suggests the possibility that such tensions are not reflected in earnings premiums because of the weak contribution of formal education in LAC to the skills needed by modern competitive firms.

The Structure and Dynamics of Skills in LAC[1]

This section presents additional evidence on trends in skill demand in LAC. Shifting the focus from the measures of years of schooling at different levels that were presented in chapter 3, it approaches the skill content of the labor force from a labor market perspective, which focuses on the tasks performed by workers and the skills needed to perform them. The skill content of the labor force is determined by the technologies used in production processes. As technology evolves, new occupations appear and the required skill mix is constantly changing. Globally, new occupations with high demand for analytical and interpersonal skills are becoming more prevalent, while occupations that were intensive in repetitive tasks are increasingly being performed by computers.

In a well-known study, Autor, Levy, and Murnane (2003) have characterized the skill content of the labor force for the United States and analyzed its changes over the past 50 years. Their analysis documents the rise of *nonroutine cognitive analytical* and *nonroutine cognitive interpersonal* skills, which they call *new economy skills*, and a decline in routine cognitive, routine manual, and nonroutine manual physical skills. They relate this evolution to the introduction of computers and argue that it has contributed to the secular increase in the premium for tertiary education in the United States. They conclude that there is a need to further adapt the U.S. educational system to teaching the new economy skills.

This section expands the analysis of Autor, Levy, and Murnane (2003) to a group of LAC countries. The evidence suggests that weaknesses in the business environment and limited education attainment may have affected the ability of LAC economies to embark on technologies that require the new economy skills. If true, this fact would put a worrying nuance on the finding of chapter 3, which suggested that skill supply has begun to outstrip skill demand. It might be that the limitations in skill availability have pushed the region toward a suboptimal technological path where high-level skills are not in great demand.

The analysis is presented in two parts. First, we assess the penetration of new economy skills in LAC by evaluating the skill content of work for Brazil, Costa Rica, El Salvador, Mexico, and Nicaragua. Then we analyze recent trends in the skill content in Brazil, Costa Rica, and Nicaragua and discuss the role of education attainment as a possible driver in the evolution of the skill content of work.

Identifying Skills in the Labor Force

To find the skills demanded by particular occupations in the United States, Autor, Levy, and Murnane (2003) employed the skill structure identified in the *Dictionary of Occupational Titles* (DOT) created by the Employment and Training Administration of the U.S. Department of Labor (USDOL/ETA). Nowadays, the DOT is outdated and has been superseded by the *Occupational Information Network* (O*NET), published as well by the USDOL/ETA. The O*Net presents detailed information on hundreds of standardized and occupation-specific descriptors. It also provides the basis for our Career Exploration Tools, a set of valuable assessment instruments for workers and students looking to find or change careers.

Each occupation is defined by the importance of a different set of tasks (measured in a scale of 1 to 5 to denote increase in the level of importance for particular skills). These tasks are then grouped by Autor, Levy, and Murnane (2003) into five broad skill categories: nonroutine cognitive analytical, nonroutine cognitive interpersonal, routine cognitive, routine manual, and nonroutine manual physical. Table 5.1 presents the five skill definitions, as well as the tasks considered per skill.

Skill Content of Work in LAC

To replicate the analysis for the Latin American context, we employ the skill structure as defined by the O*NET. Although there may be differences in the skill content of occupations in different countries, the use of a standard classification of occupations and their skill content allows for systematic cross-country comparisons.

Static analysis. This analysis presents the current skill content of the tasks undertaken by the labor force in Brazil, Costa Rica, El Salvador, Mexico, and Nicaragua, based on the structure of occupation as presented in the most recent available household survey. The United States is added to the analysis as a benchmark. The results suggest important differences in the skill content of work across countries in LAC and show that there remains a large gap compared with the skills structure of the United States. The LAC countries (table 5.2) can be separated into two groups: Brazil, Costa Rica, and Mexico have a larger content of analytical, interpersonal, and routine cognitive skills, whereas El Salvador and Nicaragua have a larger content of routine manual and nonroutine manual physical skills. The first group has a larger content of new economy skills, but it is still below U.S. levels.[2]

Dynamic analysis. The analysis focuses on Brazil, Costa Rica, and Nicaragua, for which we were able to characterize occupations[3] across time[4] (figure 5.1). In Brazil, we observed changes over roughly 30 years, between 1981 and 2009. In that period, routine cognitive skills increased in importance. This increase may reflect a population increasingly located in urban areas and the emergence of more manufacturing jobs. In marked contrast with the United States, the analytical and interpersonal content of the labor force registered a slight decline. Finally, as in the United States, the manual content decreased.

In Costa Rica and Nicaragua, the analysis is restricted to a nine-year period. Costa Rica shows an impressive expansion in the analytical skill content of the labor force during this period, which is likely related to the

Table 5.1 Skill Categories of Work

Skills	Nonroutine Cognitive Analytical	Nonroutine Cognitive Interpersonal	Routine Cognitive	Routine Manual	Nonroutine Manual Physical
Sub-skills	• Analyzing data or information • Thinking creatively • Interpreting information for others	• Establishing and maintaining personal relationships • Guiding, directing, and motivating subordinates • Coaching and developing others	• Repeating the same tasks • Being exact or accurate • Handling structured vs. unstructured work (reverse)	• Working at a pace determined by speed of equipment • Controlling machines and processes • Spending time making repetitive motions	• Operating vehicles, mechanized devices, or equipment • Spending time using hands to handle, control, or feel objects, tools, or controls • Using manual dexterity • Having spatial orientation

Source: Acemoglu and Autor 2011.

Table 5.2   Distribution of Skills in LAC and U.S. Labor Forces

	United States	Brazil (2009)	Costa Rica (2008)	El Salvador (2009)	Mexico (2010)	Nicaragua (2009)
Nonroutine cognitive analytical	3.04	2.81	2.80	2.65	2.76	2.66
Nonroutine cognitive interpersonal	3.10	2.95	2.95	2.86	2.95	2.90
Routine cognitive	3.13	3.05	3.03	2.99	2.94	2.93
Routine manual	2.47	2.63	2.72	2.70	2.63	2.76
Nonroutine manual physical	2.31	2.55	2.58	2.62	2.60	2.70

Source: Authors' elaboration based on household surveys in years indicated.
Note: Scale of 1 to 5 is used. A score of 5 denotes high importance of skill.

Figure 5.1   Dynamic Trends in Skill Distribution in Brazil, Costa Rica, and Nicaragua Compared with the United States

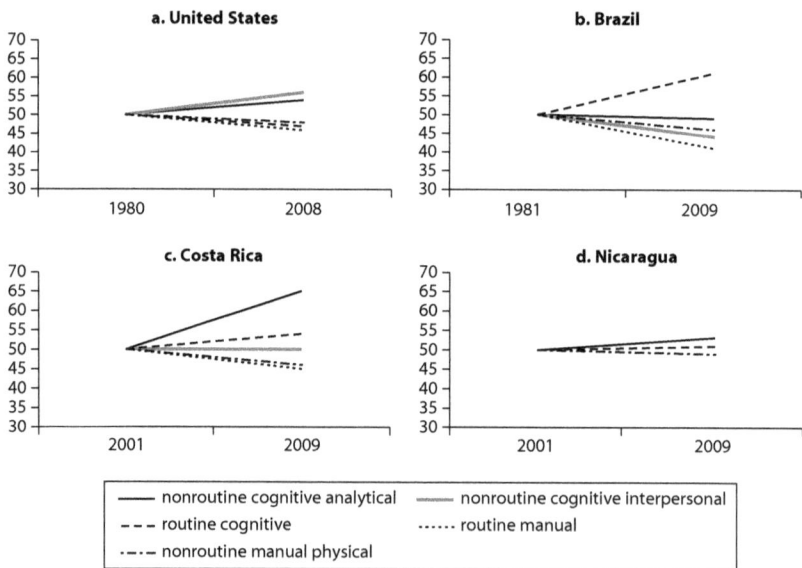

Source: Authors' elaboration based on household surveys from Brazil (1981, 2009), Costa Rica (2001, 2008), and Nicaragua (2001, 2009); United States data from Census of the Population 1980 and 2008.

country turning into a technological hub in the region. But the other new economy skill—nonroutine cognitive interpersonal—has remained relatively stable. The weight of manual skills in the labor force decreased. In Nicaragua, the skill structure remained unchanged, probably reflecting the lack of dynamism of the economy.

Relationship between the Evolution of Skill Content and Quality of Education

The capacity of the economy to absorb technological change depends on the capacity of the labor force to adapt to the new skills required by the new technologies and on the overall business environment and investment climate. Higher levels and better quality of education will enable individuals to adapt to new technologies, be retrained, and so forth. To assess the relationship between education and labor market skill content, a twofold approach is followed. First, we assess the skill content of work done by migrants from each country to the United States and evaluate how it correlates with objective measures of the quality of the education system in their country of origin. Second, we follow cohorts with different levels of education and assess how fast they adapt to technological change. Figure 5.2 plots the skill content of work done by migrants to the United States with tertiary education against the quality of their country's education system, proxied by the score obtained in the Second Regional Comparative and Explanatory Study (SERCE)[5] test in sixth grade. There is a clear positive relationship between the quality of the education system in their country of origin and the new economy skill content of the occupations that individuals perform in the United States.[6]

We next analyze how groups with different education levels migrate toward the new economy skills over time. We followed the cohort born in 1970 in Brazil between 1992 and 2009, separating individuals with primary, secondary, and tertiary education. Table 5.3 presents the evolution, focusing on analytical skills. Those with primary education experienced a decline in the analytical content, while those with tertiary and secondary education increased the analytical skill content of their work.

We conclude that technological development, through the incorporation of computers, has dramatically changed the bundle of skills potentially demanded in the labor market. Those countries with a labor force able to perform the new economy skills have engaged faster with these technologies, allowing their citizens to access better jobs. LAC countries have a generally low component of new economy skills in the labor force, but there are important differences within the region, in terms of both stocks and dynamics. The incapacity of LAC to increase the new economy skill content of work may be related to low-quality education and unfavorable business environments. The analysis shows that education plays an important part in the acquisition of skills. Better-quality education would likely enable the region to move toward better jobs, with higher content of new economy skills.

Figure 5.2   Correlation of Education Quality in Migrants' Country of Origin with Skill Content of Work Done in the United States

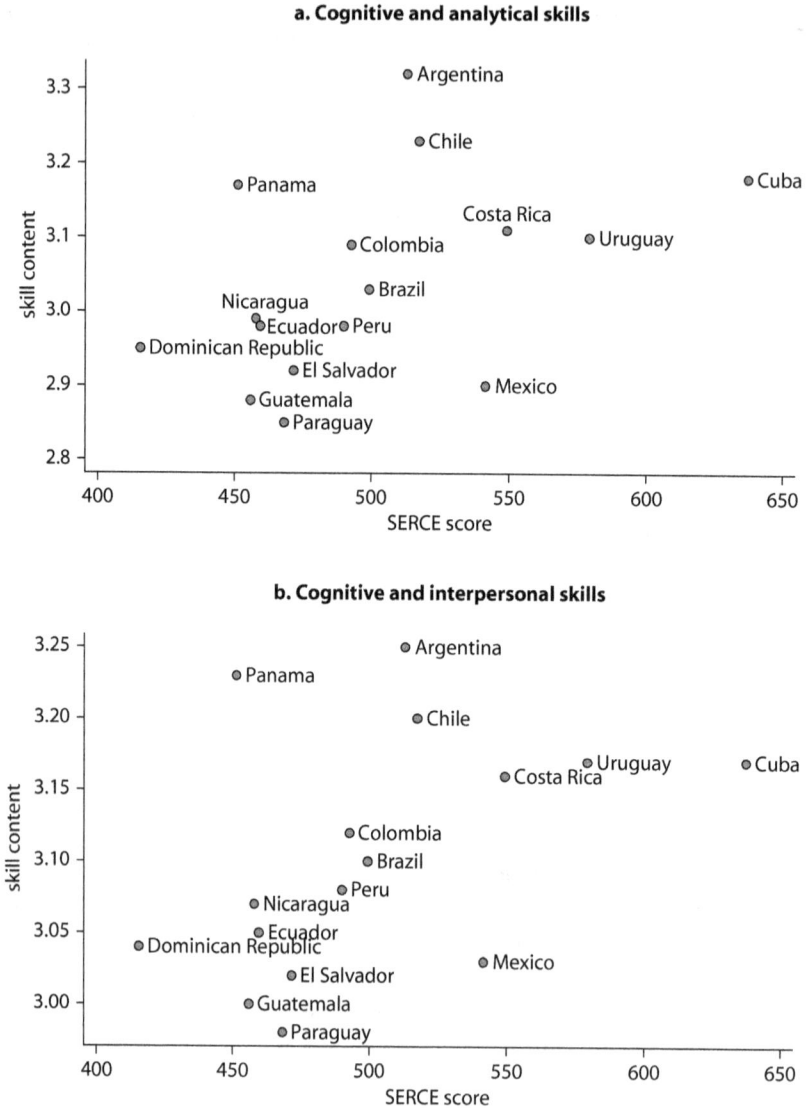

a. Cognitive and analytical skills

b. Cognitive and interpersonal skills

Source: Authors' elaboration, based on Luque and Moreno 2011.
Note: Skill content is assessed on a scale of 1 to 5; quality of education is assessed by SERCE score; only individuals with tertiary education are included.

Table 5.3   Trends in Nonroutine Cognitive Analytical Content of Work for the 1970 Cohort Born in Brazil, by Education Level

	1992–95	1996–2000	2001–05	2006–09
Primary	50	50	43	40
Secondary	50	56	60	59
Tertiary	50	63	69	68

Source: Authors' elaboration based on household surveys.

Technology Adoption and the Demand for Skills in LAC: What Can We Learn from the Time Taken to Fill Job Vacancies?[7]

In the previous section, we saw that the skill content of work in LAC has developed differently from that in the United States over the past quarter-century, with much less expansion of the occupations using high-level "new economy" skills. We concluded that this fact could reflect an accommodation of the pattern of development to labor supply constraints. This conclusion would suggest that the region's education and training systems should improve the production of workers able to carry out such functions. In this section, we present additional evidence that tends to support this hypothesis, based on the analysis of the recruitment lags experienced by relatively sophisticated LAC firms, using data from the World Bank Enterprise Surveys.

In recent decades, as a result of liberalization and globalization, LAC has developed a significant sector of firms that are incorporated into international markets and linked to increasing adoption and adaptation of technology. We used cross-country and regional variation in the time taken to fill job vacancies by such firms to explore the hypothesis that this process might be hampered by labor supply constraints, limiting their growth.

We compare the average time taken to fill a job vacancy for firms that differ in their degree of global integration in external markets or in the adoption and adaptation of technology but are otherwise similar. Our findings show that technology adoption or adaptation is strongly linked to demand for skilled labor, which is relatively scarce. Furthermore, there is evidence that this effect may severely constrain firm growth and productivity.

There is opinion survey evidence of shortages of workers with relevant skills for the available jobs in most countries (figure 5.3). It is likely that this shortage disproportionally affects dynamic firms that must continually

Figure 5.3 Share of Firms Reporting Skills as an Obstacle, by Country and Region

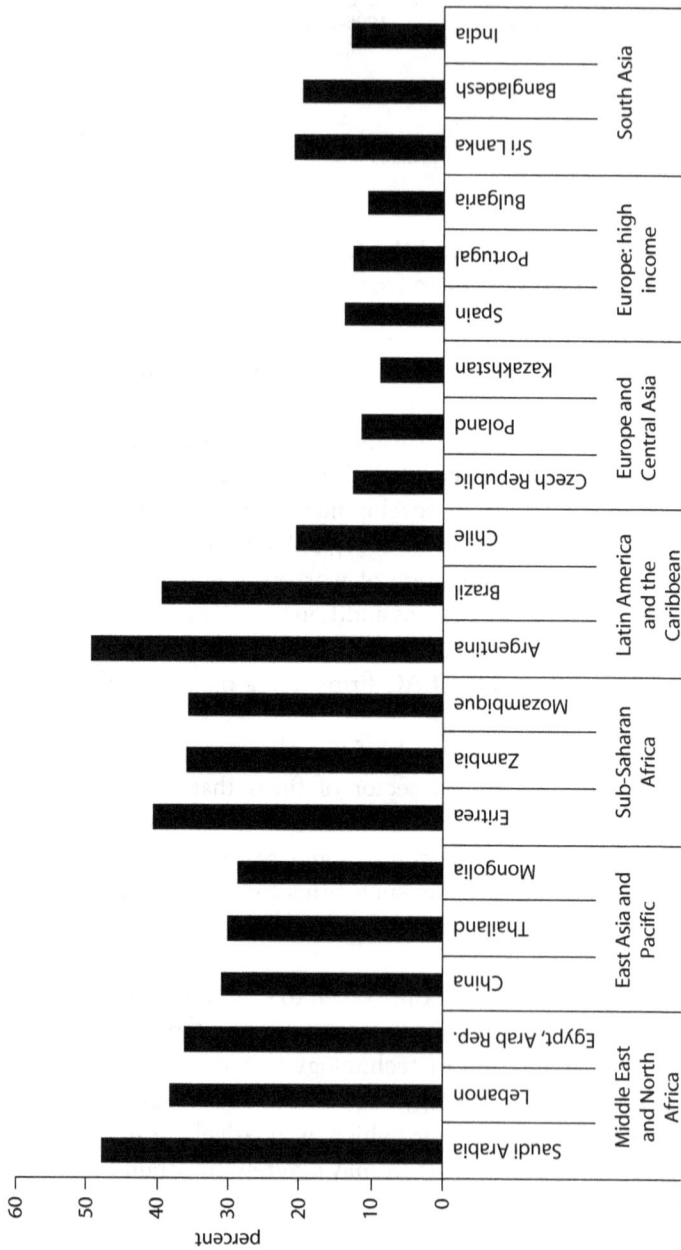

Source: World Bank Enterprise Survey.

adjust their workforce to new technologies and organizational structures to remain competitive. If so, this shortage may hamper their productivity and growth. However, opinion data are often hard to interpret. Our analysis is based on a dataset from a large firm—The World Bank Enterprise Survey—that collects detailed firm-level information, including the time taken to fill a job vacancy for skilled and unskilled workers.[8] This sort of information on objective constraints is likely to be a more consistent measure of problems with skills than the firm's opinion about skill constraints.

The Enterprise Survey has data for seven LAC countries: Brazil, Costa Rica, El Salvador, Guatemala, Guyana, Honduras, and Nicaragua. The surveys were conducted between 2002 and 2007. The sample was designed to be representative of the main sectors in each country. Only one wave of data per country is included in our sample (the most recent wave). The dataset includes information on the average time taken to fill a job vacancy (skilled and unskilled), labor earnings to skilled and unskilled workers, and average job turnover.[9] It also includes many other characteristics of the firm, including the degree of integration into global markets—proxied by exports, imports, and foreign direct investment—as well as on each firm's technology adoption practices.

We explore the variation in the number of weeks to fill a job vacancy at the firm level to assess the degree of skill mismatching in the labor market. This number indicates the efficiency of the labor market.[10] When long periods are taken to fill vacancies, it may be a sign that the skills and competencies of available workers do not match the technical requirements of the unfilled jobs. Job vacancies could also proxy matching problems between firms and workers, linked to low effort in job search or failures in the firms' recruitment strategies. Another possibility is sluggish adjustment between supply and demand because of occupational or geographical immobility (for example, local costs such as housing or high reservation wages among the unemployed).[11]

We compare within-country variation in the time taken to fill an external vacancy for firms located in the same narrowly defined labor market, so that supply-side factors and regulatory factors are controlled for. We then consider if more globally integrated firms and those adopting technology more frequently take longer to fill vacancies. If so, the shortages of skills may be an obstacle to their growth.[12]

Vacancies take longer to fill in LAC than anywhere else in the world, for both skilled and unskilled workers (figure 5.4). On average, employers in Latin America take almost four weeks to fill a job vacancy with external

Figure 5.4   Average Time to Fill Job Vacancy, Regions of the World

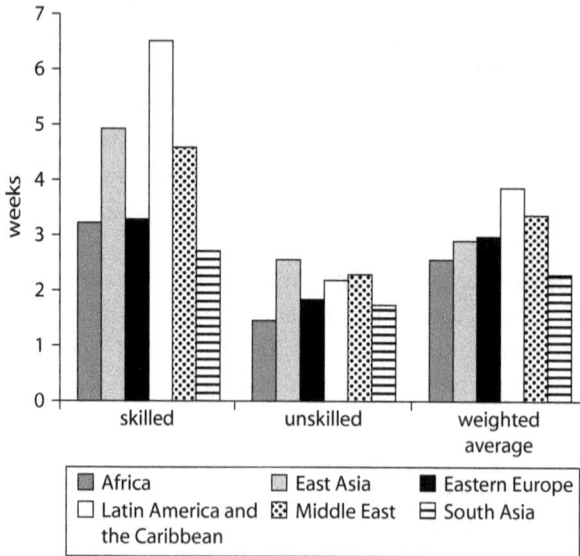

Source: Authors, based on Almeida and Jesus 2011.

candidates. This figure compares with less than three weeks for Africa and South Asia. These cross-regional differences are likely to be related not only to the composition of firms in the country and their demand for skills, but also to the composition of skills in the population and the stringency and enforcement of hiring and other labor regulations.[13]

Firms take longer to fill job vacancies for skilled than for unskilled workers. Figure 5.5 shows that the time to fill a job vacancy is about three times longer for skilled than for unskilled workers. On average, firms take 2.1 weeks to fill a vacancy for unskilled labor, and 6.5 weeks for skilled labor. This difference is likely related to the fact that firing and other costs of labor are greater for skilled workers, so that a more thorough screening of candidates is needed. Another explanation is that skilled workers can perform skilled and unskilled jobs, but unskilled workers can only do unskilled jobs (Albrecht and Vroman 2002). The hiring of overqualified labor into unskilled positions may shorten the time required to fill these positions relative to skilled positions.

There is robust evidence that, within each country, firms that are engaging more frequently in technology adoption and that are more integrated into global markets take longer to fill job vacancies. The same happens for more open firms. Figure 5.6 shows that there is strong correlation between time to fill job vacancies and technology adoption.[14]

Figure 5.5   Average Time to Fill Job Vacancy, Selected LAC Countries

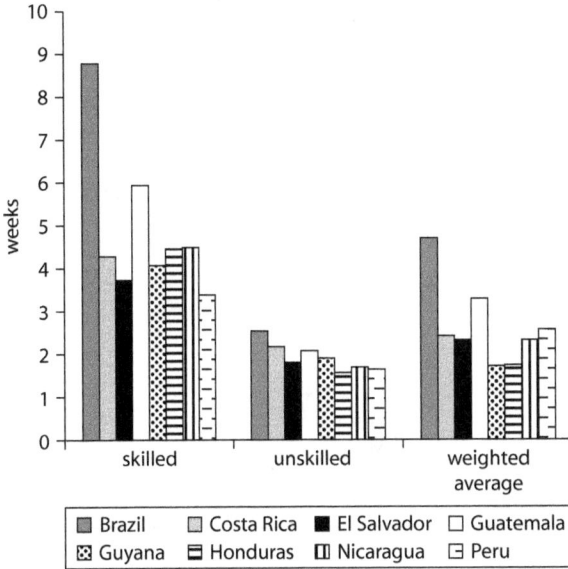

Source: Authors, based on Almeida and Jesus 2011.

Figure 5.6   Average Weeks to Fill Job Vacancy, by Firm's Innovation Status, Selected LAC Countries

Source: Authors, based on Almeida and Jesus 2011.
Note: The baseline specification is column 1. Our baseline specification controls for differences in firms' characteristics. We control for the size of firms, their age, whether the firm is owned by the government, and the share of skilled workers in the firm. We also control for specific effect of sector of activity and geographic characteristics (country and city fixed effects).

Econometric analysis confirms that the greater difficulty in hiring for technologically innovative firms is robust to differences across firms in observable characteristics, including proxies for job quality (table 5.4). The magnitude of the effects is large: firms adopting technology have a

Table 5.4   Determinants of Time Taken to Fill Job Vacancy, Pooled Regressions, LAC

	(1)	(2)	(3)	(4)
Technological innnovation	0.811***	0.811***	0.825***	0.815***
	[0.043]	[0.043]	[0.044]	[0.045]
Open	0.908*	0.923	0.916*	0.913*
	[0.047]	[0.048]	[0.048]	[0.049]
Share of skilled workers	0.525***	0.532***	0.525***	0.520***
	[0.037]	[0.037]	[0.037]	[0.037]
Mangerial education level		0.860***		
		[0.041]		
Access to finance			0.961	
			[0.040]	
Union membership				0.966
				[0.049]
Basic firm characteristics?	Yes	Yes	Yes	Yes
Industry fixed effects?	Yes	Yes	Yes	Yes
Country fixed effects?	Yes	Yes	Yes	Yes
City fixed effects?	Yes	Yes	Yes	Yes
Observations	2,569	2,566	2,535	2,448

Source: Authors' calculations based on Enterprise Surveys, World Bank.
Note: Dependent variable is the weighted average of time necessary to fill a skilled and unskilled vacancy. We use the Cox Partial Likelihood Method to estimate the coefficients. The coefficients are in hazard ratio form. Standard errors in brackets. Basic firm characteristics include dummies for firm size, age, or public ownership.
* = significant at 10%; ** = significant at 5%; *** = significant at 1%

20 percent lower probability of filling a job vacancy, while more open firms have a 10 percent lower probability. The differences remain strong after controlling for differences across managerial education, access to finance, or the degree of unionization (which could, in turn, lead to a firm's higher selectivity in searching for the best worker matches).[14] Because we always control for country and city fixed effects, we believe that firms reasonably face the same labor supply, but, if anything, these firms are more likely to face more candidates for any given vacancy because they may offer better job quality. This fact would lead us to estimate a *lower bound* for the real effects of technology on the demand for skills in Latin America.

Difficulties in hiring are present for both skilled and unskilled workers. Our findings show that, all else being constant, firms adopting technology more frequently and with more openness are still 15 percent and 7 percent, respectively, less likely to fill job vacancies even for unskilled workers.[15]

We conclude that the technical skills demanded by more high-tech industries, such as knowledge of English and information technology, are likely important factors constraining hiring in the region. The findings show that high-level technical skills are missing. The high-tech industries—including autos and auto components, chemicals and pharmaceuticals, electronics, and metals and machinery—take even longer to fill job vacancies than low-tech industries (both for skilled and unskilled workers). We also find larger mismatches for firms that rely more heavily on some specific technologies or production processes, including International Organization for Standardization certification, research and development, or use of the Internet and computers.

Notes

1. This section is based on a background paper by Javier Luque and Martin Moreno (2011).

2. It is noteworthy that the new economy skill content of work in Brazil in 2009 is below that of the United States in 1980.

3. Many countries have changed the way they classify occupations, and we have not been able to obtain codebooks with equivalencies among them. New countries will be added as they become available.

4. The metric employed is the change in the relative position of the median between the base and the final year. There is an individual median for each skill, and the skill content for median individuals differs across countries.

5. SERCE is a standardized score taken by most Latin American countries. It is administered by the United Nations Educational, Scientific and Cultural Organization–Chile.

6. It is important that this analysis does not control for other factors that may be affecting migration decisions or legal challenges of migrants once they arrive in the United States.

7. This section is based on a background paper by Rita Almeida and Jaime Jesus, which is an extract from the paper "Demand for Skills and Skills Mismatches in the Developing World: Evidence from Job Vacancies."

8. Almeida and Jesus (2011) explore a large cross-country firm-level dataset across more than 13,000 firms located in 46 developing countries. In this section, we look more in-depth at the seven countries in LAC.

9. The specific question asked on vacancies was: "Within the last two years, how much time (in weeks) did it take to fill out your most recent vacancy through external recruitment for a skilled technician and for a production/service worker?"

10. There is a large amount of theoretical literature looking at the determinants of job matching (for example, Albrecht, Navarro, and Vroman 2009; Albrecht and Vroman 2002; Mortensen and Pissarides 1994).

11. All these explanations are likely to be complementary (rather than competing) hypotheses for the existence of "jobs without workers" and "workers without jobs."

12. Our findings are constrained by the lack of time series information and by the greater focus on formal sector manufacturing firms. Although the sample does not collect time series information in most variables of interest, it collects a rich set of firm characteristics that are immediately comparable across several countries, usually unobserved in most administrative datasets. This information is useful for conducting several robustness checks and addressing omitted variables and reverse causality arguments. The nonrepresentativeness of the nonmanufacturing sectors may also be a concern. This characteristic is a limitation of this book, because there is some anecdotal evidence that the increase in the demand for skills has been stronger for services than for manufacturing.

13. We investigated this cross-country correlation for the sample of LAC countries in our sample using the Doing Business indicators for hiring and firing. We find a positive, although statistically insignificant, correlation between the stringency of hiring regulations and the average time to fill a job vacancy. Also interestingly, the correlation between the difficulty of firing workers and the average time to fill a vacancy is negative in LAC. This fact suggests that it is easier for employers to fill a job vacancy when it is harder to fire the employee (which may capture the effect of job quality).

14. Although not reported, we also tested the robustness of our findings to differences in wages and incidence of job training (available on request).

15. This correlation is robust to the inclusion of country and sector fixed effects, as well as other firm characteristics like size and age of the firm, degree of public ownership, and proxy for the education of the workforce. Interestingly, we find strong evidence that job vacancies take longer to fill in larger firms and those with a more educated workforce.

References

Acemoglu, Daron, and David Autor. 2011. "Skills, Tasks, and Technologies: Implications for Employment and Earnings." *Handbook of Labor Economics*, 4 (B): 1043–171.

Albrecht, James, Lucas Navarro, and Susan Vroman. 2009. "Efficiency in a Search and Matching Model with Endogenous Participation." Discussion Paper 4097, Institute for the Study of Labor, Bonn.

Albrecht, James, and Susan Vroman. 2002. "A Matching Model with Endogenous Skill Requirements." *International Economic Review* 43 (1): 283–305.

Almeida, Rita, and Jaime Jesus Filho. 2011. "Demand for Skills and the Degree of Mismatches: Evidence from Job Vacancies in the Developing World." Unpublished manuscript, World Bank, Washington, DC.

Autor, David, Frank Levy, and Richard Murnane. 2003. "The Skill Content of Recent Technological Change: An Empirical Exploration." *The Quarterly Journal of Economics* 118 (4).

Luque, Javier, and Martin Moreno. 2011. "Skills in the Labor Force in LAC: Current Structure and Recent Dynamics." Report to the World Bank for Background Paper FY10, World Bank, Washington, DC.

Mortensen, Dale, and Christopher Pissarides. 1994. "Job Creation and Job Destruction in the Theory of Unemployment." *Review of Economic Studies* 61: 397–415.

Murnane, Richard J., and Frank Levy. 1996. *Teaching the New Basic Skills: Principles for Educating Children to Thrive in a Changing Economy.* Cambridge, MA: The Free Press.

CHAPTER 6

Conclusions

This book has reviewed the expansion of educational attainment (years of schooling) among the emerging labor force in Latin America and the Caribbean (LAC) and analyzed its impact on educational achievement (such as test scores) and on labor market outcomes (earnings). To the extent feasible and given the type of evidence available, we then analyzed the causal factors underlying the observed trends to draw interferences about their possible developmental significance. In this final chapter, we present a summary of the main findings and the agenda for future work that have emerged from the study.

Many of the findings of this book are very positive.

First, we find that education attainment (years of schooling) has improved markedly across LAC over the past two decades.

Second, average achievement (learning outcomes) has also been getting somewhat better, in spite of the fact that many more disadvantaged students are being drawn into the system.

Third, we also find that declining education earnings premiums, which have been observed in the region's labor markets over the past decade, most likely reflect a slowing of the relative growth of demand for skills, and not a deteriorating quality of those skills. Another factor contributing to declining premiums is the role of minimum wages in many countries in compressing earnings distributions and reducing the earnings premiums for secondary education. Other studies have shown that the shifting distribution in favor of low-skilled workers has contributed to reduced poverty and better (more equal) income distribution (lower Gini coefficients).

Fourth, although tertiary earnings premiums have recently started to decline, they remain high enough to stimulate continued growth in household demand for tertiary education. Because tertiary coverage in many LAC countries remains well below the Organisation for Economic Co-operation and Development (OECD) mean, this fact will facilitate the possibility of a continued catch-up in the region's educational profile.

Nevertheless, we also report findings that should give policy makers pause. Other regions (such as East Asia) have expanded their education attainment even faster and are still reporting rising earnings premiums, suggesting that their graduates might be more economically valuable than those of LAC. The Program for International Student Assessment (PISA) data underline the huge gap that exists between the learning achievement of secondary students in LAC and OECD countries (equal to about two years of education at age 15).

This achievement gap is a huge challenge and, at the same time, an enormous opportunity. If LAC can catch up with the OECD on PISA scores, it can reap a benefit in enhanced productivity and growth potential. However, the recent positive trends in achievement have been modest. The analysis presented in this report shows that they are linked to efficiency gains (improved grade-age correspondence) that cannot continue indefinitely, while learning achievement within specific grade levels is scarcely improving and may even be deteriorating.

There is also worrying evidence that the occupational pattern of skill use in the region is moving on a disparate path from that of advanced economies. LAC is expanding less in areas that (in the United States) have been shown to require sophisticated *new economy* skills, such as high-level analytical and interpersonal skills. This finding is reinforced by evidence from enterprise surveys of long lags in recruitment of skilled workers among firms that are inserted in global economic relationships (exporters and innovators). These findings suggest that, notwithstanding the overall decline in education earnings premiums, skill constraints might still be restricting the region's growth and threatening to consign much of LAC to the second tier in the global economy.

We conclude that the region needs to do more to improve the quality and relevance of its education and training programs at secondary and postsecondary levels. This, in turn, requires policies to reinforce links to the labor market. An important dimension of this effort is the need to strengthen regulatory systems and improve the quality of information available to students and funders on the performance of institutions and the outcomes for the beneficiaries.

One clear gap in the information needed to optimize spending decisions concerns the links from specific skills to labor market outcomes and life outcomes. There is a need for good-quality household survey data on the links between education, skill sets, and outcomes. The next phase of this study will begin to address this challenge through new labor force surveys in three LAC countries (Bolivia, Colombia, and El Salvador). These surveys form part of a global effort, led by the World Bank, to improve the understanding of skills to promote employment and productivity. They will collect labor force data on educational histories, employment, earnings, skill endowments (literacy, numeracy, and social literacy skills), dimensions of personality, and attitudes to time and risk that might be relevant to labor market outcomes. The resulting data will deepen the understanding of the open questions, identified in this book, regarding which skills are most needed to facilitate faster future growth of employment, productivity, and earnings in LAC.

At the same time, potential students (who are thinking about investing their time and money in tertiary education) and policy makers (who are thinking about subsidizing them) know too little about the quality of the programs offered and the likely outcomes if those students graduate successfully. The problem is general and spans all types of tertiary education. There are already significant advances under way to improve the regulation of university systems in many countries in the region. An immediate challenge is to establish a similar dynamic in the regulation of nonuniversity tertiary education, or technical vocational education and training (TVET). The next phase of this study will address this issue by rolling out an evaluation framework for TVET that was developed and piloted in Argentina during this first phase.

www.ingramcontent.com/pod-product-compliance
Lightning Source LLC
Chambersburg PA
CBHW070406200326
41518CB00011B/2080